If this life be not a real fight, in which something is eternally gained for the universe by success, it is no better than a game of private theatricals from which one may withdraw at will. But it feels *like a real fight.*

William James

Colleges & Universities As Agents Of Social Change

College Self Study Institute, 10th

Edited by

W. John Minter

and

Ian M. Thompson

Center for Research and Development in Higher Education,

University of California, Berkeley

and

Western Interstate Commission for Higher Education

University East Campus, Boulder, Colorado 80302

November, 1968

Additional copies available. $3.50

FOREWORD

The Western Interstate Commission for Higher Education and the Center for Research and Development in Higher Education, Berkeley, present here the papers of the Tenth Annual College Self-Study Institute. Since 1960, the Commission has joined with the Center to co-sponsor institutes in a number of areas of interest to administrators in higher education.

The purpose of the institute is to present significant research findings and informed opinion to college administrators and public officials concerned with the broad and fundamental issues in higher education. The institute also affords opportunity for dialogue among administrators and researchers which stimulates further study in critical areas of higher education.

The contributions of the authors of these papers and of the Center and WICHE staff in planning and conducting these institutes, we gratefully acknowledge.

Leland L. Medsker, Director
Center for Research and Development
in Higher Education, Berkeley

Robert H. Kroepsch, Executive
Director, Western Interstate
Commission for Higher Education

November, 1968
Boulder, Colorado

63939

PREFACE

The title theme of this book was first selected to be the theme of the institute at which the papers were presented. The selection of the theme involved members of the staffs of both WICHE and the Center for Research and Development in Higher Education at Berkeley. Two members of the center staff were then among the faculty of the institute, and their papers are contained herein.

It is always the object of these two higher education organizations to select a topic which will be relevant in the immediate future but also about which enough will be known and have been experienced that the resulting papers are more than mere speculation. It is always hoped that the papers will contain clear signals suggesting and guiding future research in higher education and that they will help administrators deal wisely with the changes which are so rapidly transforming the contemporary environment.

There are always many more persons who make significant contributions to this series of books than are mentioned. To simply list those many names here would not show adequate appreciation for the efforts which they have contributed. Though one unique and difficult contribution does call for recognition—it is that of Mrs. Dorothy Buck of the WICHE staff. It is Mrs. Buck who takes the works of a number of diverse and independent thinkers and skillfully welds them together in such a way that the end product might truthfully be called a book.

W. JOHN MINTER
IAN M. THOMPSON
Editors

CONTENTS

Colleges & Universities As Agents of Social Change

PRECIS

The relationship between (the university and its environment) is now so intimate that the university may be in danger of losing its essential character and of becoming the pawn in a bitter struggle for power among social, economic, and political forces which would capture and use it to their own ends.

This does not mean that the university should look inward, that its teaching and research should be irrelevant to the social problems, dislocations, conflicts, and confusions of the world around it. But it does not necessarily follow that the university qua university should mount a direct campaign to change the social order—that it should march into the market place, into the ghetto, or into the governmental arena at the head of the political and social forces dedicated to social reform.

The institution works indirectly by making the results of scholarship and research freely available to individuals and organizations engaged in a wide variety of social, cultural, economic, and political activities. The university will change society through individuals rather than through corporate action.

Is there a touchstone by which the university's essential character and the conditions and limits of its implication in social reform can be tested? It is the maintenance of intellectual freedom. If the intellectually free university disappears, the free society will likewise perish.

COLLEGES AND UNIVERSITIES AS AGENTS OF SOCIAL CHANGE: AN INTRODUCTION

T.R. McCONNELL

PROFESSOR OF HIGHER EDUCATION

CENTER FOR RESEARCH AND DEVELOPMENT IN HIGHER

EDUCATION, UNIVERSITY OF CALIFORNIA, BERKELEY

*T*he "ivory tower" is an outmoded figure. In fact, neither the college nor the university has ever been completely isolated socially. The membrane separating the institution from its environment has always been a more or less permeable one. But the boundary between the university and its surroundings has become increasingly ill defined, and there is constant interchange between them. The relationship is now so intimate that the university may be in danger of losing its essential character and of becoming the pawn in a bitter struggle for power among social, economic, and political forces which would capture and use it to their own ends.

That the university has an obligation for public service is no longer in question. The points at issue are the ways in which it is appropriate for the university to serve society. The most controversial issue for discussion at this conference is whether the college or university should serve as an instrument of direct social action.

Academic cloister or social activist?

In the report of a discussion by the trustees of the Carnegie Foundation for the Advancement of Teaching on "The University at the Service of Society," two diametrically opposed positions with respect to the university as an agent of social change were identified. One extreme was stated as follows:

> . . . the university . . . should abjure any conception of itself as an activist shaper of the larger society. It should not "bite off propositions," develop "positions," or be a "protagonist" for causes. It should stick to the pursuits of the academic cloister with which it has traditionally been concerned and carry them out to the best of its ability. All else in the end is illusory.

The opposite position was described in this wise:

> . . . among all institutions in the nation, the university has the greatest responsibility to be a shaper of the society. As such it has an obligation to identify social wrongs and take an aggressive lead in rectifying them. It must be engaged, activist, reformist . . . .

> In this view, the university can best protect its position not by an attitude of aloofness from the great social issues of the day but by actively engaging in them. And this kind of activist role, far from detracting from the traditional functions of teaching and research, will actually strengthen them.[1]

At stake in the resolution of these two positions is the conception and maintenance of the university's essential purpose. Chancellor Roger Heyns has declared that the primary purpose of the university is intellectuall ". . . intellectual pursuits and intellectual discourse are, above all others . . . the values of a university." He went on to say that the function of the university is to develop new truth, not new ideologies, and that ". . . intellectual discourse is preferred over action generated in moments of passion."[2]

This does not mean, presumably, that the university should always look inward, that its teaching and research should be irrelevant to the social problems, dislocations, conflicts, and confusion of the world around it. President Samuel B. Gould of the State University of New York has asserted that, on the contrary, by its very nature the university must examine and question the status quo, comment freely on its shortcomings, and explore alternatives for social action.[3] But it does not necessarily follow that the university *qua* university should mount a direct campaign to change the social order — that it should march into the market place, into the ghetto, or into the governmental arena at the head of the political and social forces dedicated to social reform. The conservative position is that institutionally the university should make its impact on social conditions indirectly.

The institution works indirectly, first of all, by making the results of scholarship and research freely available to individuals and organizations engaged in a wide variety of social, cultural, economic, and political activities. Second, the university will change society through individuals rather than through corporate action. "Out from its citadel will go educated men and women with a passion to remake the world," said the Carnegie Foundation trustees. "From it will emanate ideas and knowledge that will be revolutionary in their impact. This will be public service in its truest form."[4]

The university: partisan or nonpartisan?

Associated with the position that the university should serve society indirectly is the attitude that the institution itself should be nonpartisan on public issues. President Nathan M. Pusey of Harvard has declared that that university does not take political stands except on matters that affect its own well being.[5]

Perhaps no college or university in the United States has a more activist group of students and faculty than Antioch College. But this institution, too, recently asserted its corporate neutrality on social issues and social action. A committee composed of five students and five faculty members recently proposed "that Antioch College shall not take an institutional stand on the war in Vietnam and that we remind ourselves that the only proper institutional stands for the College are on issues scrupulously defined as educational."[6] The committee said that it took this position, among other reasons, because it wished "to comply with the Antioch Civil Liberties Code in its clear intent: to free individual advocacy from any shadow of institutional orthodoxy and to prevent as skillfully as possible any identification of a partisan action with an institutional position."[7]

The Antioch committee also argued that the public will profit more from divided academic counsel than from a single

3

corporate voice. The committee declared that corporate non-partisanship should contribute to the achievement and maintenance of "a genuine community of free individuals" in which "dissent is fostered, not nervously tolerated, and where controversy is creatively managed."[8]

The partisan university

In sharp contrast to the nonpartisan position taken at Antioch, the School of Social Welfare at Berkeley recently took a public stand against the Vietnam War, the first faculty at Berkeley to take such a position. The faculty added its voice to that of the National Association of Social Workers, which had urged a halt in bombing, a cease-fire, and peace talks. The faculty resolution stated that:

> Our country's Vietnam policies give lie to the commitment to people implicit in our roles as social work educators. Our professional efforts are rendered futile and pitifully absurd by the tragedy of American and Vietnamese military casualties, the enormity and horror of the Vietnamese civilian casualties, and the demoralization of the American people.[9]

For a professional society to take a public stand on such an issue as the Vietnam War would seem to many to be a defensible action. Is it equally defensible for a university professional school to take an official position on what has become a political as well as a moral issue? Perhaps the crucial test of the appropriateness of such action is whether or not its effect will be to discourage or engender student and faculty dissent, to stimulate or to inhibit unprejudiced investigation of public issues and welfare problems, in a word, to enhance rather than to erode intellectual freedom in the university.

If faculty members are to remain free to investigate any subject, and to express freely the results of their research and reflection, said Capen, one of the most uncompromising advocates of academic freedom in American higher education, the institution itself must remain neutral. He wrote:

> We ask immunity from interference in order that we may single-mindedly perform these tasks which are vital to the

welfare and progress of society. If society is to have faith in our loyalty to the cause of truth, it must never have occasion to suspect that that loyalty is divided.[10]

The university: passionate and involved

In any event, student activists are skeptical that an institution which is aloof and intellectual rather than committed and passionate will have a very serious impact on the country's festering sores that cry out for human compassion, righteous indignation, retribution, repudiation, or destruction of the status quo, and forthright social reconstruction. Poverty, discrimination, injustice, denial of freedom and human dignity, and immoral warfare, they say, demand action, not scholarly detachment. They assert that to change these conditions demands a crusade, not a trip to the library. They want to find the scholar in the city, not in his study.

Many students are suspicious of the aloof and nonpartisan intellect, which, they say, easily becomes the juiceless mind, a mind without esthetic awareness and emotional drive.[11] But, one might ask, does anyone really believe that it is necessary for intellectual processes to crowd out esthetic or humane sensibilities, or, on the other hand, for emotion to displace reason? Would it not be more appropriate to say that if education is to enable young people to cope with the problems which beset society, it should neither be devoid of passion nor sparing of intellect? Is not the problem we face that of submitting emotion to reason and of coupling intellectual solutions with feeling and commitment?

Surely all institutions today are committed to protect the rights of students and faculty members as individuals, or the right of voluntary associations of students or faculty members freely to engage in legal social action. But if universities *qua* universities become partisan and contentious, they may lose their intellectual freedom and their very great degree of self-government, together with the ability to protect the rights and freedoms of their individual members. Dr. Buell G. Gallagher has been quoted as having said that:

Wherever men of conscience and good will are confronted by the organized efforts of contentious and angry partisanship—

5

the search for truth is in grave danger. And within the groves of Academe this means that no man is safe or secure. It means the end of academic freedom and the beginning of the reign of unreason.[12]

Possible consequences of politicizing the university

If colleges and universities identify themselves with particular political causes, no matter how just they may be, may they not find themselves also politicized in wholly unexpected and intellectually disastrous ways? Lepawsky asked:

If their political role is allowed to escalate, how can their members dissuade the body politic within the greater society from scrutinizing their supposedly intellectual conduct and from throwing into the balance the political counterweight of other groups or interests who claim to be threatened by the academicians?[13]

Conservative or right-wing political groups, though now relatively quiet, may come to power in the university and, observed Lepawsky, "take active steps toward changing the political complexion of the academic establishment. If they did not, it would be one of the most remarkable cases of political abstinence in history."[14] Universities may be especially vulnerable to external political forces. Enroused citizens or an angry legislature may inflict serious damage on a public institution by determined efforts to curb intellectual inquiry, free expression, and open advocacy.

Universities already engaged: for whom?

The perceptive observer might declare that it is purely academic to ask whether the universities should be engaged in social action; they are in fact already heavily involved in countless ways. Two examples may suffice to make the point.

Through their experiment stations and extension divisions, the land-grant colleges and universities over the years have assumed direct responsibility for improving agricultural production and for reshaping the agricultural economy. They are now immersed in the process of revolutionizing agricultural technology. The University of California has developed a new strain of tough-skinned tomatoes and invented the machinery to harvest them. In doing so, the university contributed to the loss of many jobs for the already disadvantaged farm laborers in the great central valley of California. Should the university accept any responsibility for retraining workers for other jobs or helping them transfer to other industries?

Two writers in the *New Republic* recently reported that the University of California has applied for a patent on a machine that may make it possible within five years to harvest mechanically most of the wine grapes grown in the state. Farm operators may profit enormously since it was said that labor costs, which now run about $20 an acre, might drop to as little as $5. The article declared that the machine model recently licensed by the university for commercial production will harvest both sides of a row of vines simultaneously, at the rate of two acres an hour, using two men to replace 70. Thousands of laborers will be displaced.[15] Does the university have an obligation to concern itself with the human beings who are displaced by the harvester it invented?

One might also ask whether it is any more inappropriate for student or faculty organizations, or the university itself, to act in the cause of peace than for the Livermore laboratory, under the joint auspices of the University of California and the Atomic Energy Commission, to engage in research and development in nuclear warfare? Or to ask whether it is any longer inappropriate for the corporate university to assist the victims of social or economic injustice to organize social, economic, or political efforts to redress the deprivation and discrimination under which they suffer?

The urban-grant university

The latter question is bound to arise if the urban-grant university espoused by Dr. Clark Kerr materializes. Kerr has proposed that the nation and the states should establish 67 urban-grant universities to stand beside its 67 land-grant universities. This institution, as he conceives it, would help rebuild and run the cities. It would send out faculty members

7

and students to show the people how to operate better urban schools, welfare and social agencies, police departments, and hospitals. The medical school would be at least as much involved in the health of the city as the land-grant university was with the health of the farmers' livestock. Members of the university community would become the chief planners of the structural, cultural, and human architecture of the city.

The urban-grant university, said Kerr, would almost certainly face a great deal of external opposition.

> There will be those, for example, who will view with apprehension the potential political alliance of the students and the ghetto dwellers. Others will fear the potential involvement of the university in partisan urban politics. . . . And so, for this university to work effectively, there will have to be a considerable amount of public understanding—especially understanding of the distinction between service based on applications of knowledge and positions taken because of partisan politics. Beyond that, the institution will need an excellent system of buffers, and this is particularly a challenge to the trustees. . . . We must bridge the gulf between the intellectual community and the surrounding society. . . . The urban-grant university can provide such a bridge and if the greater participation will result in greater controversy, we must be prepared to accept it and to deal with it.[16]

But how to deal with it he did not say.

The quasi-university service agency

Kerr has suggested the urban-grant university might organize for community service by establishing agencies corresponding to agricultural experiment stations and agricultural extension divisions. But because an institution serving the urban community will touch many more sensitive individual and social nerve endings than the land-grant university did, it may be desirable for the former to devise a new agency less directly and intimately a part of the institution than the agricultural agencies. Perhaps the prototype may be found in the quasi-nongovernmental organization, the disadvantages and advantages of which were recently discussed by the president of the Carnegie Corporation of New York.[17]

A new quasi-university organization should be funded from many sources, including federal and state governments, foundations, individuals, voluntary associations, city governments, colleges and universities, and corporations. It should be possible for faculty members to move back and forth between the agency and the educational institutions which surround it. Participation in the activities of the organization should not only enable scholars and researchers to bring their special knowledge and competence to bear on urban affairs, but also to identify problems for study and investigation. "The availability of a real laboratory rather than an abstract one, of an actual problem rather than a theoretical one, makes the university a more vigorous institution," said the Carnegie Foundation trustees.[18]

The quasi-university organization would not only provide the scholar with an opportunity for applied and basic investigation as well as social action; it would also leave him free to retire into the "inner" university for periods of reflection, teaching, and intensive research. This kind of sanctuary even the urban-grant university cannot afford to lose.

But if the university should, at times, and for some of its members, offer a haven, it should be a cloister with windows on the world. And most of the time its faculty and students will be trying to devise ways of making a better society.

In this regard Gardner finds the university seriously deficient. His criticism amounts to an indictment:

> . . . Generally speaking, when one moves from the arena of scientific and technical problems to those problems involving change in human institutions, one cannot say that the universities are a significant intellectual base for the main attack. In fact, a good many university people whose field should give them a legitimate interest in these matters barely understand what the relevant problems are. Many are debating policy alternatives left behind five years ago. Few are planning the kind of research that would sharpen policy alternatives.[19]

The test for involvement

If Gardner is right, the university is in constant danger of being both irrelevant and obsolete. But how deeply can it be engaged without compromising its primary intellectual purpose, without losing its intellectual freedom, without becom-

9

ing the pawn of any special interest group except the interest of a free society? The problems of commitment and involvement which arise when the university becomes directly embroiled in the inevitably sensitive and controversial processes of social change may not only shake its conscience, but also challenge its integrity. Is there a touchstone by which the university's essential character, its unsurrenderable value, and the conditions and limits of its implication in social reform can be tested? I think there is. I suggest that it is the maintenance of intellectual freedom. If individual freedom of students and faculty is lost, the university is destroyed. If the intellectually free university disappears, the free society will likewise perish.

[1]"The University at the Service of Society," *1966-67 Annual Report of the Carnegie Foundation for the Advancement of Teaching.* New York: the foundation, 1967, p. 8.

[2]Roger Heyns, address to the Academic Senate, Berkeley, University of California, *Campus Report* 2 (November 8, 1967) 3, 4.

[3]*Chronicle of Higher Education,* March 11, 1968.

[4]"The University at the Service of Society," *op. cit.,* p. 9.

[5]*Chronicle of Higher Education,* March 11, 1968.

[6]*Chronicle of Higher Education,* April 22, 1968.

[7]*Ibid.*

[8]*Ibid.*

[9]*The Daily Californian,* May 15, 1968.

[10]S.P. Capen, *The Management of Universities.* Buffalo, New York: Foster and Stewart Publishing Corporation, 1953, pp. 25-26.

[11]J.L. Green, "The New Student Morality," *Antioch Notes* 45:6 (March, 1968).

[12]Quoted in Kenneth Coombs, "On Academic Freedom," *Western Politica* 2 (Autumn, 1967) 18-39.

[13]Albert Lepawsky, "Academic Freedom and Political Liberty," *Science* 150 (December 17, 1965) 1559-1563.

[14]*Ibid.*

[15]Martin Roysher and Ford, Douglas, "California's Grape Pickers Will Soon Be Obsolete," *The New Republic* 10 (April 13, 1968) 11-12.

[16]Clark Kerr, "The Urban Grant University." Paper given at the Centennial Meeting of the City College of New York Chapter of Phi Beta Kappa, October 18, 1967.

[17]Alan Pifer, "The Quasi-Nongovernmental Organization," pp. 3-16 in Carnegie Corporation of New York, *Annual Report for 1967.*

[18]"The University at the Service of Society," *op. cit.*

[19] John Gardner, "Universities as Designers of the Future," *Educational Record* 48 (Fall, 1967) 315-319.

PRECIS

The university should, in deep and direct ways, recognize itself as—and act as—an agent of the most profound politics. What is wrong with the university denying modestly that it is not political and then continuing in a quiet way its role as an agent of the profound politics of modernization, reform, and freedom?

The thing wrong with universities pretending not to be agents of social change is that it is a cover-up; it camouflages the fact that universities are such agents; and in their disavowal they may fool themselves as well as others.

The federal government knows, the State Department knows, the Pentagon knows, the CIA knows, our adversaries in the world know that American universities are and have been agents for research and recruitment in support of America's present world policies and military efforts. Why shouldn't the American people and the members of the university community know the facts on this? So the official doctrine of political neutrality is wrong because it is corrupting and cowardly.

Following the truth as a question may not lead to larger appropriations for state universities. But the urgent is too often the enemy of the important, and undue prudence will not lead to good prophecy. The important thing is that we act in the faith that it is the Truth as a question that makes men free.

AGENT OF WHOM?

HARRIS L. WOFFORD, JR.

PRESIDENT

STATE UNIVERSITY COLLEGE

OLD WESTBURY, NEW YORK

When the council of our college first talked with me, one astute member asked in effect what Chancellor Heyns and I are now asked to debate, except he put it in more personal terms: "Will you spend all your time sounding off on controversial issues?" He gave civil rights as his example, but his question was really the larger one: Is it necessary and proper for a college president, or anyone representing the college, or in some cases even the college itself, to take public stands on public issues? Should the college try to change society or stick to the business of education?

I replied that I would not spend all of my time on such issues because of the demanding job they were giving me but added that, if I were in their shoes, I would worry more about someone who wouldn't spend any of his time that way, either because he didn't have anything to say or because he was afraid to say anything. A Peace Corps volunteer had goaded me: "If you become a college president, you will never say anything, sign anything, or do anything political or controversial." It seemed to me that the council of a college should want a president who would disprove that charge.

Isn't it the business of education to lead children up to manhood—to lead adolescent subjects into full citizenship? Silence, cowardice, emptiness, or nihilism at the core of the academy would be a source of corruption of the young and of society at large—the opposite of what education in citizenship should be.

This personal preface is not to suggest that what is good for a college president is necessarily good for the college. It is a short answer to the general question: Should a college or a university see itself as — and act as — an agent of social change?

Yevtushenko tells us it is man's fate to shuttle back and forth between the City of Yes and the City of No. I am glad that Chancellor Heyns and I have each been assigned one side of the proposition that colleges and universities should be agents of social change, and that mine is the City of Yes. Though there are many complicated things to say, it is good to find us standing on these strong two- and three-letter words, very short and simple words that you do not hear often enough in the academic world.

The need for involvement

Mine is an easier side of the argument because we will probably all agree that there are some occasions, involving great political and social issues, when we would all expect institutions of higher education to take sides as deeply and directly engaged agents for or against particular social changes. At least we regularly expect this of colleges and universities other than our own. As to Nazi Germany, would we not agree that the academy there had a duty to resist, with all of its individual and collective power, Hitler's laws and acts against Jews from the first forms of civil discrimination to the "final solution?" Do we not agree that universities as universities, even at the risk of their extermination, had this duty to seek to change the course of Nazi terror — that universities in Mussolini's Italy had a duty as universities to resist the Fascist oath?

Do we not believe that the academy in Greece today — as in ancient Athens — should be an agent seeking to restore the conditions of public freedom? Do we not hope that univer-

14

sities in eastern Europe will, with courage and political skill, continue to press for the liberalization of their Communist states? Do we not hope that this is happening in the Soviet Union and behind the scenes even in China?

Do we not tell universities in Asia, Africa, and Latin America to be responsible and active agents of the social revolutions necessary in most poor and newly developing nations? Do we not, through our government programs and foundation aid, in fact almost bribe some foreign universities to undertake major programs concerned with sensitive domestic social and political issues such as land reform?

How then can we take the position that universities should engage in controversial matters and be avowed agents of social change everywhere in the world but in America?

It even gets closer home than this. Those who advise against universities as universities getting involved in such issues usually stand on even narrower ground. A university president in the North may not believe that his university should risk its public or political support by involving itself directly in matters of injustice or violence nearby, a police department run amuck, or migrant workers on strike, but he is likely to believe that his counterpart in the South should risk his job and his institution by giving leadership on racial integration — and vice versa.

In fact, I suspect that most of us would agree that there are some political and social issues of such vital importance to the university that the university — even an American university — would have to act as a university, whatever the consequences. If so, then the real questions are what those issues are, how they are determined, and how the university should act. What kind of agent of change should it be?

Involvement is inevitable

Let me return to these crucial questions by another route. Mine should also be an easier side of the argument because it can be shown, I think, that any university at all worthy of that name is inevitably, whether it wants to be or not, whether it admits to being or not, an agent of social change. And if it is a powerful university, it is probably a powerful agent of social change.

This is true because of the very nature of change in the modern world — this new world ushered in by the Industrial Revolution, if not by the Renaissance, or indeed by the original Western dialectic of ancient Jews and Greeks. The world revolution of science and technology has education as its central generating source. Along with other corporations, such as business firms and states, colleges and universities are the carriers of this now nearly universal revolution of modernization.

It takes about 16 years to make a modern man — 16 years of formal education to turn an Ethiopian villager into a jet pilot, or a Nigerian bushman into a modern poet; 16 years of education for an outcaste Hindu to become a nuclear physicist, for a whole generation of Russian peasants to become skilled industrial workers, for 200 million young Chinese to learn the literacy, mathematics, and new laws of a modernizing military state. Through education, the secret has been let out that man need not be forever poor, that science and technology, economics and politics make it possible for the first time in human history for the benefits of civilization, such as they are, to be made available to the whole human race — to all men. That is the giant revolutionary fact of our time which education is making manifest.

If we look back over the history of modern civilization, we can see that universities have always been agents of change. Justice Brandeis called corporations the master instruments of civilization and put educational corporations at the heart of our corporate life, as the great shakers and movers, the most fundamental agents of change. From the days of the educating monastic corporations of the Middle Ages, which were the change agents that began to modernize agriculture — they were the first "land-grant colleges" — through the early medieval universities where "nation" was the name for a college of people from the same locality, through the great universities of the world today, our academic republics of learning have been models for — if not sometimes the mothers of — the larger republics of learning known as nation-states.

In this perspective, with the plot so clear, with colleges and universities cast as central characters in our politics, now as ever, for better and for worse, how can we hope to escape responsibility by saying, "There's nobody here but us chickens, boss!"? Some chickens!

Yet that is what so many voices in higher education seem to be saying. President Johnson's chief White House advisor on education and science, not long ago said that education is too important for us to let it get involved in political controversy. This was in explanation of his action in dropping from a White House committee a distinguished scholar, who now is on our faculty, who had taken an active stand against the war in Vietnam. Isn't the opposite closer to the truth? Politics is too important for it not to be at the center of education. Education is too political for it not to be involved in matters of great controversy.

The founder of the Hebrew university and later the first president of Israel, Dr. Chaim Weizmann, tells in his book, *Trial and Error,* how he convinced General Allenby during World War I that the founding of Hebrew university was not a political act and therefore should not be subject to the wartime ban on politics. It was just an educational institution, he assured the British commander. Years later, as he looked back on the power generated by the university and by the other educational institutions created in Palestine, Weizmann commented that, of course, it had been a political act. And I would add that what is true of the birth of a university should be true of its life and, when necessary, its death. It should, in deep and direct ways, recognize itself as — and act as — an agent of the most profound politics.

What is our problem?

If this is true, then what is our problem? What is wrong with the university denying modestly, as Weizmann did, that it is not political, and then continuing in a quiet way its role as an agent of the profound politics of modernization, reform, and freedom? Why ask for trouble? Why not stick to the business of education and get involved only in public con-

17

troversies that clearly and directly affect education? Why encourage universities to get more openly in the middle of controversial public problems?

The first thing wrong with this our present official doctrine is that it is not true — and untruth should be the last thing a university accepts. It is so untrue that even private profit-making corporations now feel it necessary to affirm that they *do* carry corporate responsibility for the common good. Few private corporations any longer dare to say that their concern is for themselves alone, that doing what is good for themselves is itself enough of a contribution to the common good. But universities still say this, and in doing so they demonstrate a self-centered closure that is the opposite of a truly open dialectic.

The second thing wrong with this approach is that it is narrow and selfish, and therefore ultimately ridiculous. Isn't it ridiculous for a great university to consider questions of the justice of a war or national conscription to be beyond the pale of academia — except insofar as or until its graduate students are in danger of being drafted? Yet that is what the conventional doctrine seems to say: a university is to be concerned about political issues only when they directly impinge on the efficient functioning of the university or the individual liberty of students and faculty. This is a long way from concern for the common good.

A third thing wrong with universities pretending not to be agents of social change is that it is a cover-up; it camouflages the fact that universities *are* such agents; and in their disavowal they may fool themselves as well as others. The federal government knows, the State Department knows, the Pentagon knows, the CIA knows, our adversaries in the world know that American universities are and have been agents for research and recruitment in support of America's present world policies and military efforts. Why shouldn't the American people and the members of the university community know the facts on this? What is wrong is that those policies and efforts may themselves be wrong; they may be just what ought to be changed. At least the question of whether these policies

18

"agent," "change," and "university." An agent has a principle he is responsible to, and change must have some criterion. Who or what is a university an agent of? What is our criterion for determining whether a particular change is good or bad?

A university is not the agent of the public, for it is often the public's opinion that most needs changing — by criticism, by Socratic goading, by education. Nor is it the agent of trustees representing that public, let alone of presidents or administrators all of whom depend for their legitimacy on the consent of several other constituencies, especially the faculty and students. And it cannot be the agent of faculties, for their special domains need especially to be stretched into universals. Nor is it the agent of students. The university, of course, needs to pay attention to where students are at, as they would say, but it also needs to challenge each generation to go where it has not been, to go where it ought to go. This generation particularly needs to be encouraged to take the deep and disciplined intellectual trips their present travels seem to be neglecting.

My alma mater's Socratic oracle, Robert Hutchins, says that the university's purpose "is to fashion the mind of the age and not be fashioned by it." And his predecessor at Chicago, William Rainey Harper, said in 1905 that universities should not be "deaf to the cry of suffering humanity" or "exclusive and shut up within themselves," but "the true university, of the future," should instead be "the prophetic interpreter of democracy, the prophet of her past, in all its vicissitudes; the prophet of her present, in all its complexity; the prophet of her future, in all its possibilities."

If a university to be a true university must above all be a prophet and, through this prophetic mission, fashion the mind of the age, then a university really has to see itself and be, to the best of its ability, an agent of the truth. In the beginning of our universities, when God and truth were synonymous, this was clear enough. We are told that God is dead, and I certainly have not found Him alive in any of the universities I have visited recently. Nor have I been to the mountaintop, at least not since leaving Ethiopia a few years ago; but yesterday

21

I rode a horse on the foothills of Mount Diablo up behind Berkeley — the Devil always has something to do with Truth — and the beauty and euphoria of that perspective emboldens me to paraphrase Santayana: there is no God but His word is being incarnated all the time, and especially in the corporations that call themselves communities of learning. A more academic word for all this is the one my Russian friend used: question. God and Truth are indeed the great question. Universities are agents of this great question — and must therefore do their best to be great questioners.

Let me come down from the heights to a more American version of this proposition. Let us settle for the Declaration of Independence definition of the truths that are America's great questions. Our revolutionary founders declared that the need and right of all men to govern themselves was self-evident. But for this prophecy to come to pass, the higher education of all citizens must become truly universal and good. That in itself calls for our colleges and universities to be massive and much better agents of change than they have ever been. And one of the changes most clearly required is that they change themselves and become much better models of a republic of learning than they are now. This new constitution-making within the academy, that will enable students as well as faculty to be citizens and not subjects, is one of the great social changes universities will need to give leadership in achieving.

Beyond the reforms needed in our own house, there are more than enough great public questions on which universities as universities need to throw light. These include the war in Vietnam, the racial crisis, urban development, the war on poverty, the matter of drugs, relations with China and the other places we can't get passports to — you name them.

If I have claimed that this side of the argument, in favor of open acceptance of a role as agents of change, is easier than the negative, let me concede that the consequences are not at all easy. Following the question where it leads inevitably leads on some occasions into trouble. A university that as a university resisted Hitler would have lost its life as a university — or would it? High authority says we may need to lose our life

22

to find it, and history tells us that ancient Athens was never more alive than when its buildings were captured and burned, and its people took to the sea, saying that their city was on ships. The great days of the early universities, Trevelyan tells us, were when universities were built of men alone.

If we accept responsibility for the university to speak and act on some issues affecting the whole body politic, we will of course have great difficulty deciding which issues and how to do it. But that is the kind of difficulty our minds and souls need to face. That is the kind of question, about the common good, that truth requires us to ask.

This spring many campus administrators were alarmed because students threatened to boycott classes, close down colleges, and assemble the community for debate on the Vietnam War. The position taken on most campuses was that the university had to stick to its business, those classes. But I have also heard of the different response by President Howard Johnson of M.I.T., who said that the Vietnam War was an issue that warranted the full attention of the university, that he for one was ready to listen to anyone who had light to throw on the question and that he would sponsor such a major confrontation. The students asked him to open the meeting and he agreed. Thousands came and the argument went on for hours. The dispute had been raised to its older title, a disputation. For days afterwards, I am told, Howard Johnson was greeted by students who told him that they never felt so proud to be a member of M.I.T. than on that day when the community as a whole, led by its official spokesman, engaged itself in seeking the truth about the Vietnam War. This is but one example of how a university should seek the truth.

All this is of course easier to say when your governor is the governor of New York and not the governor of California. Following the truth as a question may not lead to larger appropriations for state universities. But the urgent is too often the enemy of the important, and undue prudence will not lead to good prophecy. The important thing is that we act in the faith that it is Truth as a question that makes men free.

23

PRECIS

I do not believe that the university, formally as an institution, should take stands on noneducational matters. By formal action I mean formal action taken through its governing board or executive heads. I have the same opinion about official actions on noneducational matters by departments and faculties.

If the academic community chooses to use the university as a base of political action, if it tries to identify the university with its causes, and mobilize the prestige and the resources of the university to goals which it chooses, then it has made the university an important piece of political real estate. And it will follow, inevitably, that others, outside the university, will then regard its control and management as important for goals which they select.

Many efforts to get the university as an institution to identify with particular causes—opposition to the war for example—have arisen not from great moral sensitivity but from the desire to align the university with a particular position. There has been a struggle for control of the university rather than a passion for morality.

Universities have accepted endowments for foolish purposes or scholarship funds with unwise social implications. We have not been as sensitive as we might have been to the need to change these relationships. But the criteria are clear and their application has, by and large, protected the autonomy of the university and the essential freedom of its members, faculty and students alike.

THE UNIVERSITY AS AN INSTRUMENT
OF SOCIAL ACTION

ROGER W. HEYNS

CHANCELLOR

UNIVERSITY OF CALIFORNIA, BERKELEY

I accepted the invitation to speak to this group on this topic in part because of the pressure such acceptance would bring upon me to put in writing what I have come to believe. In addition to welcoming the discipline that would be required, I looked forward to having those beliefs examined and challenged by other speakers, panelists, and members of the audience.

My position on the question of the relationship of the university to social, political, and economic problems is essentially conservative. You should understand, however, that I speak from a campus which is characterized by a great deal of involvement in these problems. Thousands of our students, in connection with course work and outside classes, are teaching and tutoring children in poor communities, working in schools and social agencies. We offer courses which involve field work. Virtually all of our schools and colleges are involved with state and local government and many other social groups. In addition, our campus rules permit free discussion of all issues, and interest is not only lively but, for many of our students, this interest expresses itself in action and involvement. This state of affairs I approve of and defend.

Nevertheless, and indeed to protect this freedom, I do not believe that the university, formally as an institution, should take stands on noneducational matters. By formal official action I mean formal action taken through its governing board or executive heads. I have the same opinion about official actions on noneducational matters by departments and faculties.

Because of the ambiguity of what constitutes official institutional action, I would go further and state that the executive head must recognize that what he may believe are private acts often are interpreted as official positions. I would counsel great restraint in his own pronouncements and actions. To a lesser extent, this applies to other officers and to a lesser extent still the faculty, but in all of these, the ambiguity is real enough that people in these categories should at least recognize the import of their acts or utterances.

I refer particularly to official pronouncements, and I associate myself with the Antioch position quoted in Dr. McConnell's paper, "The only proper institutional stands . . . are on issues scrupulously defined as educational."

With respect to action, to activity or programs, using the language of the questions posed by Dr. McConnell, I believe the university makes its contribution to social conditions indirectly — "by making the results of its scholarship and research freely available" and through the free action of individuals rather than corporately. I believe it should be nonpartisan.

I take these positions for precisely the reasons given in support of them contained in the McConnell paper (although not necessarily by Dr. McConnell himself). As the Antioch group stated: The purpose of avoiding institutional positions is to free individual advocacy and choice, to preclude orthodoxy which inhibits dissent. The fundamental basis for freedom to learn and to teach has been that the position of individual faculty members and students does not reflect that of the institution as such. It is this independence that is jeopardized in many subtle ways if institutional neutrality is abridged. There is enough evidence on our campus that even an informal consensus on the war has interfered with dissent; it may have influenced the nature of scholarship; certainly attempts have been made to influence the conduct of the classroom. This interference would be infinitely greater if there had been formal institutional commitment.

Joseph Shoben, in "Toward Remedies for Restlessness: Issues in Student Unrest," says:

> . . . Academic freedom, it must be recalled, has never applied to institutions; the doctrine of *Lehrefreiheit,* for example, confers no immunities upon the university except one; the right to clothe its faculty members in a special protective armor as they explore *any* trail that may lead to truth and wisdom. In contemporary terms, it is generally accurate to say that any tenured member of any faculty is entitled to espouse any position toward the war in Southeast Asia without fear of losing his job or suffering other reprisals from the college or university at which he teaches. Like most ideals, this one sometimes is dubiously honored in the breach rather than in the observance, but cases like that of Professor Genovese at Rutgers underscore the principle here. Our central point, however, is that the condition of the institution's making this essential gift of security to its professors is that it must itself remain neutral. In a very real sense, the only commitment to a *social* value — in contrast to the academic values that guide the internal processes of scholarship, instruction, and the nature of its intra-institutional community life — that a university makes *as a university* is its intransigent commitment to academic freedom. So long as it takes no corporate stands with respect to the major controversies that beset all dynamic cultures, it can insist on the peculiar freedom of individuals to investigate, to publish, and to debate which is the cornerstone of the academic enterprise. By this insistence, it maintains an open campus on which, at least in laudable theory, *all* ideas may compete for a hearing and minority points of view can be safely maintained.

My reading of our history here in California would lead me to turn another of Dr. McConnell's questions into a statement of fact: If colleges and universities identify themselves with particular political causes, they will find themselves politicized in wholly unexpected and disastrous ways.

If the academic community chooses to use the university as a base of political action, if it tries to identify the university with its causes, and mobilize the prestige and the resources of the university to goals which it chooses, then it has made the university an important piece of political real estate. And it will follow, inevitably, that others, outside the university, will then regard its control and management as important for goals which *they select*. Our best protection against that most dreaded intervention in university autonomy — the political test of fitness for membership in the student body or faculty — is in carefully avoiding an internal test. This is what formal and informal orthodoxy really represent.

Individual self-restraint

The best protection from intervention, for the preservation of autonomy, lies in sensitivity to this risk and the practice of individual self-restraint. Professor Richard Hofstader put this eloquently in a speech on the Berkeley campus:

> The delicate thing about freedom is that while it requires restraints, it also requires that many of these restraints be self-imposed and not forced from outside. The delicate thing about the university is that it has a mixed character, that it is suspended between its position in the real world, with all its corruptions and evils and even cruelties, and the splendid world of our own imagination. The university does in fact perform certain mundane services to society — and there are those who think it should aspire to do nothing else. It does constitute a kind of free political forum — and there are those who want to convert it primarily into a center of political action. But above these aspects of its existence stands its essential character as a center of free inquiry and criticism — a thing not to be sacrificed for anything else.

> A university is not a service station. Nor is it a political society, nor a meeting place for political societies. It is, with all its limitations and failures, its fragile and compromised professors, its equivocal administrators, its tumultuous and self-righteous students, its classified research, its instruction that does not instruct, and all the other ills that institutional intellectual life is heir to, the best and most benign side of our society, insofar as that society aims to cherish the human mind.

To realize its essential character, the university has to be dependent upon something less precarious than the momentary balance of forces in society; it has to pin its faith on something that is not hard-boiled or self-regarding; it has to call not merely upon critical intelligence but upon self-criticism and self-restraint.

There is no group of professors or administrators, of taxpayers or alumni, or students, there is no class or interest in our society, that ought to consider itself exempt from bearing its costs and patiently enduring its conflicts and trials; nor is there anyone who should want to do other than rally to its generous support.

Freedom is limited

I trust that in this audience we will not attempt to fool ourselves. Many efforts to get the university as an institution to identify with particular causes — opposition to the war, for example — have arisen not from great moral sensitivity but from the desire to align the university with a particular position. There has been a struggle for control of the university rather than a passion for morality.

With those not so calculating — and there are some — it has represented a naive understanding of the pluralistic nature of the university and the essential part official neutrality plays in the freedom of us all.

The freedom that a university receives from external intervention on the part of the society that supports it is never absolute; it waxes and wanes; it is certainly not a divine right. The supporting society, whether public or private, is not required to grant absolute independence to its institutions of education. As educators we should tell the supporting society, and we do, that the greatest universities have traditionally been freest. And we should explain why this is so: because the untrammeled search for truth and its successful transmission — through learning — is most likely to be achieved with minimum constraints. We can and do tell the public why this in turn is true — because of the nature of the process of discovery and the process of learning. But when we do this we appeal to society's wisdom and its maturity and its security. We are not appealing to a bill of rights.

While there may be an ideal amount of freedom a university should have, as a practical matter it is limited. How much freedom it has is determined by the (1) degree of enlightened understanding of the society and the restraint it exercises by its procedures for resource allocation (line item budgets are, for example, more restrictive than block grants), (2) methods of selection and terms of office of board members, and (3) restraints imposed by the university upon itself.

Academic freedom and all the attendant freedoms are, therefore, never guaranteed permanently. Whether they are granted or interfered with is an educational and a political process. We try to educate the supporting society on the need for freedom — on educational grounds — in order that we can perform our essential tasks more effectively and in so doing serve the society more effectively. The process of obtaining protection, or losing it, is very often political.

We can identify some of the conditions under which the threat to essential autonomy from external intervention increases. One is inexperience on the part of the supporting public. The Stony Brook drug raid is an illustration. Another is a high state of anxiety about change. This is an extremely short-hand way of describing our present condition in America generally. Another is intense value conflict in the society on a particular issue. Activities by universities in defense were acceptable, even applauded, during World War II and, now, with an unpopular war, they have become controversial. I specify these conditions, and I admit the list ought properly to play a significant role in determining the nature of the university's involvement in particular activities.

To summarize up to this point: My central position rests on my conception of a university as an intellectual community, dedicated to training and research. It is committed to the intellect and to the use of reason, to knowledge. I then proceed to a consideration of the conditions under which these functions can best operate and, finally, to a consideration of the effect on those necessary conditions of involvement in social affairs. I have indicated that institutional commitments can have the effect themselves, under certain circumstances, of curtailing freedom and inviting external interference.

30

It should be obvious that we are dealing with matters of degree. And most of what I have said refers to statements of position.

But what about the obvious fact that the university is involved in social affairs and has made institutional commitments to programs? I would like to turn now to an examination of some of the types of involvements. I would suggest that, out of careful examination of these, we can establish some of the criteria that must be met to guide the university in establishing (or terminating, for that matter) institutional commitments. We have assembled a good deal of wisdom on this subject over the years, and it is worthwhile to make it explicit.

Before I turn to institutional commitments to programs, let me note some established institutional practices that facilitate interaction with the society that have been of tremendous usefulness to the society and to the university. Although accepted, they are not without their risks and are not without their critics both inside and outside the university.

I refer first to the advisory, consulting relationship. The university in recent years, through its pay practices, leave of absence policies, and appointment policies, has greatly increased the interaction between the society at large and individual members of the academic community. I believe that most of the federal programs in education, science, health, social welfare, and conservation, for example, have been primarily influenced by members of the university community, acting as private individuals but with the aid of institutional policies that permit and even encourage this kind of activity. It is important to observe first that the institutional practices and policies which made this easy are not coercive. Each faculty member has been free to choose to participate or not.

Second, there are implicit or explicit educational considerations which are taken into account. It is expected, particularly with respect to consulting relationships, that the experiences contribute to personal growth and, therefore, educational effectiveness. The academic community must get a return.

31

Leaves of absence are evaluated in terms of this effect on the teaching and research function of the university in addition to the external criterion of service in the public interest.

Another form of university participation, which involves university policy and practice, is individual grants and contract research. Here again, the emphasis is on the relationship between the individual faculty member and the sponsor. Whether or not the research occurs is primarily a matter of whether the individual applies for the grant. But institutional policies and practices have enormously facilitated the frequency and ease of these transactions. Universities have set up offices to perform services for these contracts, provided space for most of them, and created new categories of employees that these projects needed.

This institutional posture of commitment can't be hidden under the rug. Nor should its value in making the university effective in social change be ignored. The university responsibility is there. Indeed, as far as the federal government is concerned, these grants are awarded to the university and the university is held responsible not only for fiscal matters but also for the quality of the work done. There are, at least when we are at our best, educational considerations which determine what kind of grants are sought. They must provide freedom for the investigator, permit publication of findings, contribute to the education of students and the development of staff. They must also be in harmony with educational development goals of the institution.

I turn now to another form of participation involving institutional commitment: the establishment of units of the university structure that have a programmatic mission. The Radiation Laboratories here, the Lincoln Laboratories at M.I.T., Argonne Laboratories at the University of Chicago, and the Willow Run Laboratories at the University of Michigan are examples. Here the university, by contractual arrangement, undertakes to establish and maintain a research facility. Not all of these I have mentioned have the same relationships to the university involved or to the sponsor. These relationships have also altered during the years, but in general they have been characterized by a certain degree of separation from the other units of the university—in management and personnel policy. They might better be called university-affiliated units. These have begun with a public need for a particular kind of activity and a requirement for the kind of personnel and environment that a university can provide.

The needs and requirements of the university have influenced the decision about whether the relationship is to be established and its nature, if the decision is affirmative. Usually, these facilities represent research tools that are beyond the capacity of the university to develop. In the days after the war, there was a disposition to establish these programmatic units in federal laboratories away from and separate from campuses. The NIH laboratories in Bethesda are illustrations. Many of us tried to turn this tide, believing that in many instances the educational functions, particularly graduate training and research, would be harmed if federal laboratories became the exclusive pattern. If universities were to be on the frontiers of certain areas of discovery, it was necessary that these facilities be near and affiliated with universities. We also argued, I think successfully, that the research itself would be done better.

Over a period of time these relationships have been altered in the interests of further educational objectives: the free dissemination of research findings, active participation by faculty in the direction of the program, involvement of graduate students, and so on.

Another form of institutional commitment to programmatic research and training has involved institutes and centers in such fields as mental health, social research, labor and industrial relations, and agriculture. Here again, the university assumes some obligation over and above the commitment of specific individuals to carry on a particular effort. The same criteria apply, although the decisions are a little less controversial primarily because usually there is no specific partner or enduring cosponsor.

All of these devices have greatly increased the university's involvement in our social life. This involvement has been to the profit, by and large, of both the community and the university. Primarily educational considerations have determined *whether* they should exist and how they should function. Finally, we should not forget that these activities have always involved us in controversy with the external community in one way or another, at one time or another.

Examination of the effectiveness of group health care programs in Windsor, Canada, by the University of Michigan Public Health School, experimentation with flouridation by the University of Michigan Dentistry School, studies of police in Oakland by the Center for the Study of Law and Society — innumerable other illustrations could be cited of some degree of public clamor over this sort of participation.

These activities have been defended and protected by (1) the general reputation of the university for objectivity, (2) the range of such activities governing many areas that the university engaged in, (3) the obvious relationship of these activities to the research function of the university and, finally but not insignificantly, (4) the posture of the investigators themselves. They resolutely limited their role to that of investigators and, even though they had a right as citizens to do otherwise, they did not become political protagonists. The importance of these subtle differences in posture cannot be overestimated.

But what about training and service activities? Here we must be reminded particularly that we are not dealing with an all or none phenomenon, with whether or not the university should be involved, but rather to what degree. Since the areas of possible involvement are more controversial, the sensitivity becomes all the greater. Here again we are not without experience and wisdom that must come to our aid as we move, as we most certainly will, into new areas of involvement — as, for example, in President Hitch's program of commitment to involving the university in the urban crisis.

Let's turn first to training programs. First of all, we must remember that even in such well established programs as law, medicine, architecture, and public health, there is always a state of controversy between the faculty and the profession. Typically the profession and often the public at large are critical of the lack of so-called practical emphasis. Sometimes there has been criticism about the attitudes and values communicated by the school. We have learned that the educational program, content, and pedagogical method, must be in the hands of the university faculty for better or for worse. Our faculties have learned that there must be a reasonable fit between the program and the demands of the practicing profession, but the determination of that optimum fit is really theirs.

We have also had controversies over whether or not there should be a particular training program. Whether optometrists or morticians or labor leaders or journalists should be trained in universities has been the subject of considerable debate and uncertainty from time to time. In general, we have asked ourselves the following questions before deciding to go ahead:

1. Can anyone else do it better?
2. Is there a body of content, a discipline to be learned?
3. Does the program draw on as well as enrich other programs? All, again, educational questions.

Since many institutions are beginning to experiment with courses and programs which involve field work (in part as a way of meeting the criticism of the lack of relevance of the educational experience on the part of students) and since these departures will inevitably involve academic units that have not had experience with this kind of training, it is worthwhile to examine what we have learned from our experiences in more established programs which involve field work, internships, etc., as part of the training. I remind you that we have had a great deal — in medicine, dentistry, public health, social work, and education. Here are some of the lessons as I read them:

1. To obtain optimum results, the university must have a great deal of control of the field situation. The students must be geared into the agency to be sure that they aren't just additional manpower, or given routine assignments; real op-

portunities for learning must be provided. Close supervision is required, often requiring additional staff.

2. Nonetheless, by and large we have not found it worthwhile to operate the field agency ourselves. Universities have pretty much abandoned their own elementary and secondary laboratory schools. We have greatly increased our use of regular hospitals for medical education as opposed to developing our own. I doubt whether, even in our new medical schools, we will ever again establish large general service hospitals. And even the ones we still operate are different, or ought to be, from general community hospitals operating under other auspices. Patients in university hospitals expect to be treated by students; they must expect to be subjects for research. The university hospitals are expected to limit referrals to those cases that contribute to education and research in contrast to taking everyone who needs health care. Private practice use of facilities is absent or limited.

These are matters of degree, but the emphasis is clear. We are not in the business of operating social agencies. I could go on with this complicated topic, but I want to mention one little-noticed but very real objection to university-operated and university-run social agencies: the autonomy of the community itself may be compromised. We should be just as sensitive to the ability of the community to determine the kinds of services it wants as we are to protecting our own freedom.

3. The practicum learning experience must be related to the on-campus learning. The relation between theory and practice is complicated, and great attention must be given to the complexities. The classroom learning must inform practice and vice versa. Mere uninterpreted experience is not enough.

4. The guiding concept for student behavior and experience is that he is a student — not a general citizen, not another member of the troops, and not an employee.

What about strictly service activities? These haven't been many and properly so. I think this is primarily because of the application of these criteria. We have not been, and we should not be, service stations. We have generally tried to select those service activities which were subject to our controls, those which met the requirements of the academy and which contributed to the educational functions.

It is important, as I list these considerations, to recognize that there are and ought to be individual differences among institutions. They differ in function, in student body, in the social climate in which they live, and in countless other ways. A possible service activity might offer great opportunities for training to one institution and little to another. On the other hand, an institution may develop such a rarified atmosphere with respect to its surroundings that its well being becomes a matter of supreme indifference to the supporting community. Such a university may seize opportunity to serve in order to change this institutional posture that would not be selected somewhere else.

I mentioned earlier that one criterion for participation was: Can another institution do it as well or better? I want to expand on this idea briefly. There is a great deal of sentiment that the university should involve itself in all worthy causes, attack all important problems primarily because it has enormous resources and can do it. I believe this view has serious defects. Edward Levi recently put this very well in *Chicago Today:*

> . . . Universities are among the important institutions in our society, but there are other important institutions. You will recall de Tocqueville's description: "Americans of all ages, all conditions, and all dispositions constantly form associations. They have not only commercial and manufacturing companies, in which all take part, but associations of a thousand other kinds, religious, moral, serious, futile, general or restricted, enormous or diminutive." The fact that there is an unmet need does not at all mean that a university is best equipped to take it on. Even if it is, the added function may place such a burden upon an institution as to defeat its basic purposes. Even a welfare-indoctrinated society must make choices. It may be that new types of institutions are required; it does not follow that universities should become these new types. A university which claims to be all things to all people, or as many different groups wish it to be, is deceitful or foolish or both.

37

Summary

I have tried to suggest that the question of university participation in social affairs has arisen with new force primarily
because of the war, race, and poverty, and also because of the
pressure for new pedagogical programs. It is not a new question, however. Universities have some criteria that have serv-
ed in the past and will continue to serve in the future. There
is no question that the university has and will involve itself.
Participation always involves risks. This doesn't mean that
the university should not participate but rather that the degree
of risk must be evaluated in terms of the gains for the essential
functions of a university. Clarity about these essential purposes and clear assessment of the impact on them of any involvement will provide the greatest protection from unwarrant-
ed interference.

In spite of the fact that I believe our record here is not bad,
I don't want to leave the impression that it is without blemish.
Universities have accepted endowments for foolish purposes
or scholarship funds with unwise social implications. We have
not been as sensitive as we might to the need to change these
relationships. But the criteria are clear and their application
has, by and large, protected the autonomy of the university
and the essential freedom of its members, faculty and students
alike.

PRECIS

How can the university retain the freedom it requires from a society it criticizes? How can it retain its competence and its capacity to affect the course of society without incurring hostility from a society content with its course? There is where the crunch comes. The sleeping issue is now shouting at us.

Since some kind of balance will be required, opinion will inevitably enter into the striking of such balance. Burdened with that admitted subjectivity, certain guidelines, certain bounds not to be overstepped, may be suggested as a means of provoking thought as to where the balance should be and how attained.

(1) The university must not compromise its integrity.
(2) The university must maintain a distinction between corporate and individual views and acts.
(3) The university must be free to do whatever it takes to keep relevant in its age.
(4) The university must not lose its identity.
(5) The university must not lose its critical capacity.
(6) The university must not seek legal power or the power to coerce.
(7) The university must not deny its accountability.

One would hope to see, as a stabilizing but adaptive influence in an agitated age, the collaboration of a responsible but responsive university and a tolerant society. It takes both.

THE TIGHTENING TENSION:
THE UNIVERSITY'S EXTERNAL RELATIONS

ELDON L. JOHNSON

VICE-PRESIDENT

UNIVERSITY OF ILLINOIS, URBANA

A dynamic tension between the university and its environment is normal, but the current face-off between university and public is cause for concern. The trend is even ominous. Society is becoming more avaricious and demanding in its consumption of university services. The university is becoming more willing to put down its walls, to be where the action is, to criticize public policy, and even to risk confusing power with influence. This mutual interpenetration creates more points of friction and more promise of conflict.

The central issue

The central issue is not new. Whether the freedom enjoyed within the campus can be extended outside the campus bothered universities centuries ago. Social criticism and public service as university functions have been growing for almost a century. Catering to clients as well as to students and serving as the arm of government have been respectable land-grant university traditions. Whether freedom of action extends as far as freedom of thought, and whether professors enjoy the same latitude off the campus as on, have long troubled the academic waters.

When is a campus a legitimate sanctuary and when a revolutionary cell? When does sponsored research seduce the university? How far should the university be the agent of government? When can the university countenance the disobeying of the law? Is neutrality really an endorsement of a rotten society? All or most of these questions were current before contemporary students added their flamboyant provocation. Whether these youth are the "new fascisti," nihilists, or genuine agents of change, they evoke images of what is inside the walls, ready to spill out on an innocent society when the university talks of its extramural mission. Political forays, disruption, violence, and other direct actionism from universities in Europe and Latin America have etched the image more deeply.

But the underlying issue persists: How can the university retain the freedom it requires from a society it criticizes? How can it retain its competence and its capacity to affect the course of society without incurring hostility from a society content with its course? There is where the crunch comes. The sleeping issue is now shouting at us.

The slender thread

The university exists on the sufferance of the state. As Karl Jaspers has said: "Its existence is dependent on political considerations. It can only live where and as the state desires . . . . Society wants the university because it feels that the pure service of truth somewhere within its orbit serves its own interests." But the service of God is offensive to the devil. The pursuit of truth inevitably leads to controversy about both the truth and its consequences. Hence it is not surprising to note that Professor Walter. P. Metzger, historian of academic freedom, concludes that it takes great vision for "any society, interested in the immediate goals of solidarity and self-preservation," to subsidize free criticism and inquiry. The accommodation which persists in our universities is "one of the remarkable achievements of man," although "one cannot but be appalled at the slender thread by which it hangs."

In this precarious balance, society has come to adopt some pragmatic tolerances. It is accustomed to extension activities, to service bureaus, to contractual relations with government, and to overseas assistance. The pre-Civil War college related only modestly to the limited professional life of that time and not at all to science, technology, business, and agriculture. In contrast, higher education today is actively serving these, plus government itself, on a host of fronts, and with public acceptance. But the "slender thread" begins to appear when unorthodox or politically sensitive activities are attempted, even under these tolerances—activities such as university implementation of the U. S. Department of Agriculture's social policies, dispensing of contraceptives in the university medical clinics, service overseas for the CIA, leadership training for civil rights workers, or urban renewal assistance.

The slender thread is further attenuated when faculty and students resort, as some are now advocating, to a host of direct action measures to challenge "the establishment," to appeal to "the higher law" of conscience, and to dramatize social ills thought to be too extreme to wait upon persuasion. Indeed the object has sometimes become precisely that of straining the tolerances of society; and that can easily be done by anti-war stances, formally adopted manifestos for social reform, preferential graduate admissions of draft resisters, occupation and obstruction of public buildings, insistence on fixed quotas for the employment of minority groups, defiance of the police, memorializing for "pot" and "pill," aiding Cuba, making alliances with the black nationalists, and doing much else which anyone can add from his own home experience. These are the shouts and sharp blows of the Karate Age, as someone has called it, perhaps unwittingly to contrast it to the whimperings of the so-called Aspirin Age of two decades ago.

What are the stakes in this new confrontation? What is placed in jeopardy? Most obviously, the freedom of the university itself from outside interference. Prior to that, society's acceptance of the university as an objective intellectual force, possessed of integrity and competent to be a social critic. Most directly at stake is the survival of the activist role the university community professes; but more importantly, at stake is the university's moderate and necessary participative social role which is required for maintaining relevance in what it teaches, what it investigates, and what it extends to the outside world. The hard-to-defend jeopardizes the defensible. At stake is the whole interconnecting apparatus between the university and society, the apparatus through which meaningful communication takes place, balance is attained, accommodation is achieved, and mutual dependence is acknowledged.

Audiences to consider

Who is affected? Who gets involved? Who produces the consequences? Four audiences or potential respondents may be identified: the external academic world, the mass media, the general public, and the government.

The external academic community consists of the lower educational institutions, other universities and their faculties, professional societies, and accrediting bodies. This is such an "in" group, so sympathetic and understanding, that it would rarely present any consequences or sanctions. An exception might arise from one of the professional societies which takes its cue from its practitioners and feels possessive about the educational production of the members' new colleagues and competitors. Accrediting bodies, unlike the general public, would probably regard extreme institutional activism as an acceptable additive unless it patently threatened to disrupt and despoil the teaching and research functions. Extreme university activism might alienate counsellors in high schools and junior colleges, with enrollment effects; but, generally speaking, the fellow educators would be hard to alienate and, hence, are not a source of major concern.

The next audience, the mass media, is a vital concern. Its impact is great. It goes about its professional job, as it sees it, paying little or no attention to the consequences, but leaving that to the public in the way that science leaves its capacity for evil as well as good. Virtually every opportunity the university has to reach the general public, as distinguished from selected groups like the alumni, is through the mass media. This includes what the university itself supplies, what reporters dig up, or what unexpectedly explodes into newsworthiness, however much the explosion might have been engineered precisely to capture headlines. Since the nature of news— except that concerning the political, social, business, athletic,

44

and entertainment elites—is that which is aberrant, unusual, extreme, or unrepeatable, social activism on the part of the university, or its faculty or students, is likely to get unusual coverage. Such activism produces adversary relations, on which journalism thrives. The approach usually is, What is the score? Who is winning?

Paradoxically, the university is also a communications institution. Its success depends on the free flow of ideas in the scholarly community, and among scholars outside, with only minor spill-over to the general public. However, the trend toward more activism and more direct outside involvement inevitably puts the university into the arena covered by mass communications rather than by scholarly discourse. So the university will become increasingly subject to the major limitation of the mass media: the necessary presentation of selective evidence.

Complex problems, which activist positions usually represent, inevitably suffer when stripped to simplistic interpretations, overcompression, or one-facet coverage. Likewise, the university which is tied to the complex problems also suffers as the reading or listening public makes up its mind on the basis of inadequate perception. Getting the facts is no doubt a scrupulously-held journalistic objective, but space dictates selectivity and readership dictates appeal to the mass. Ample examples show how the ripple can be made a tide, the amusing made menacing, the minority made a majority, the conscientious made unconscionable, and the compromise made a capitulation.

When to these natural news limitations of the mass media are added the editorial policies of commentators and publishers—policies based on their own news coverage plus their personal predilections—the university must seriously reckon with this pervasive prism, yielding both color and heat, which stands between it and its other publics. No conceivable crisis of activism can escape the influence of public scrutiny via press, radio, and television. No one has. No one will. This is the price an activist university must be prepared to pay. It may win journalistic allies or enemies, but it will not be ignored.

Another maker of consequences is the general public—all readers and listeners of the mass media, including the alumni, the benefactors, the consumers (such as extension clients, contractors, and parents of students), and those who are uninterested and unaffected until some university act or policy welds them into some new pro- or anti-university "public." This is the most potent university audience, in one sense, but it is also an object of much democratic folklore. It makes public opinion. It helps evaluate what ought to become public policy. It dictates to government. But it cannot rise above the sources of its information, which for the individual reader or listener is not only selective but largely monopolized. It is subject, as Walter Lippmann used to say, to the pictures in the head—not only the accumulated encrustation of values and prejudices through which all supposed fact is screened but also the pictures which are newly being built by the persistent impact of the news media. In this context, the university is what the public *thinks* it is. Fact is not as important as the perception of fact, unless one can find some independent way to appeal to fact, to make it real again.

Within *"the* public" are subordinate publics, some closely allied to the university and with which it may have special ways of maintaining the liaison—such as alumni publications, special releases to select lists, offices concentrated on benefactions, and communications with the professional groups standing behind the university's professional schools. But the more important question is what makes a "public" for the university. Such a group has to arise out of a perceived interest— maybe a threat, maybe a cause to join—which is keenly enough felt to inspire action. This public-generating capacity exists in unusual degree in activist programs. This is where the patriotic groups are galvanized into action, the interest groups become defensive, the power-threatened retaliate, the neighborhood reacts to the intruding university, the outraged religious sects are heard from, and the forgotten group is inspired to shout. It is only a step from the birth of such publics to their appeal to public action through public officers, for punishment or for favor.

This brings us to the last and most potent maker of con-

46

sequences: government. Whether public or private, this is where the university meets its greatest potential enemy, as it may likewise be a potential benefactor. Government can change the rules of the game or call for a new game. Its restraint is what makes the university possible: its not doing what it clearly could do. Therefore, the university which wants to participate in matters the government also cares about, the great public policy questions, will have to take the government very much into account—government as an ally, as a supporter, as a protector; or as a score-evener, as an enemy, as an intruder, as a seducer. The university will have to measure its moderation/aggression scale alongside the government's tolerance/retaliation scale. This means local, state, and national governments, and the executive, legislative, and judicial branches. All levels and all branches have recently demonstrated their capacity to embarrass, to restrain, and to punish higher education if the provocation is deemed sufficient.

Some possible consequences

Having looked at three particularly potent university "publics," we should now ask, What consequences can these makers of consequences produce?

The mass media can obviously help manufacture all the other publics; but they can also themselves oppose bond issues, create "mass protests," seek governmental intervention, distort the university (and student and faculty) image, and create the smoke by which gullible people know there is fire. It would be a great disservice to the mass media to impute the worst motives to all; but, regrettably, one can find examples of editor-politician combinations which have attempted to whipsaw universities into complete ideological subjugation, first by driving professors back into their temple and then by cleansing the temple. This aggression breeds its own retribution, indeed among other mass media, but often after the damage has become almost irreparable.

The general public, with its innumerable voluntary associations, has many ways of producing consequences the university must reckon with. Withholding money is one potent

47

weapon. Colleges can withstand it in theory and often do, with great flourish. They can even withstand it in practice, if it is not too much. However, activist programs which have brought faculty and students into vigorous defiance of the law have demonstrated that there is no accredited college or university in America so liberal in its orientation that the alumni and other benefactors will accept such defiance without verbal and financial retaliation. The provocation may have to be great, and the college officials may defend the policies or programs, but the hard fact of inevitable consequences has to be weighed in the balance—consequences which say, "There *are* bounds, and we think you are skirting or exceeding them." Parents of students or potential students have the same options and sometimes exercise them.

The most powerful public influence lies in another direction — in its capacity to influence government and to create new public policy. Every legislator has his political antenna up, and even judges and police chiefs follow the papers and the election returns. They are all helped by the interest groups who memorialize the public officials, write letters, buttonhole, and threaten. These range from the Daughters of the American Revolution to the Maoist factions, and from the National Association of Manufacturers to the Audubon Society. If the university wants to follow a tough line, the general public can be noisy but largely impotent, until it begins to speak through government.

Government has a whole arsenal of weapons, from threat to overkill. Here is where that modicum of truth in the ancient opposition to federal aid comes home to haunt us: as government has become a larger benefactor, it has gained larger capacity to injure by withdrawing its favors. Ironically, that argument was usually made by those who would have been least likely to incur public disfavor by policy disagreement. While the federal government has great and growing power to damage by withdrawal of its support, it has no ready means of singling out particular institutions. It can set standards and deny favors to those who fall short, but it has no direct appropriating capacity to retaliate as a state legislature has, and sometimes uses, over its state institutions.

The power of enforcing standards as a condition of financial support is currently illustrated by federal legislative amendments to bar funds to faculty and students who have been convicted of rioting on or off campus or who have willfully violated a lawful campus rule or regulation. The prohibitions could be extended to cover many other publicly offensive actions. An angry government, particularly a state government vis-a-vis a state institution, has a wide range of fiscal restraints and harassments it can employ against the offending university, if the stakes are high enough.

Other governmental devices are police action; investigations, substantive or audit; legislative changes by statutes and by riders; admonitions in committee hearings or reports; hortatory resolutions; and formal public statements, executive or legislative. Not to be overlooked is another vast area: the intrusion of the courts into university affairs on the initiative of both private citizens and public officials. The litigious era has now hit higher education. The net effect has clearly been restrictive on the institution. Whether the university is contemplating an activist course or reacting to one in progress, it can no longer overlook how its actions may appear in the courts. The judicial bodies, or any other of these external publics, have great capacity to agitate what might be called "the public mix," creating compounded and reinforced effects, to the serious detriment of the university. For example, the Fayette County Grand Jury in Kentucky recently put three publics on the back of "the persons in authority at the university" by asking the Board of Trustees to "develop . . . an attitude more compatible with the desires of the alumni and general public."

Some guidelines for universities

So we come back to the troublesome question: how can the university continue to push society toward adaptation without suffering crippling reprisal against its freedom to push? The university has the intellectual power. The public, through government, has the legal power. How can the latter be moved by the former?

Perhaps the answer is: not at all without risks and without occasional deadlocks. Some way must be found short of surrender by either party. Society can surely find a rational ordering of its critical needs for both legal compulsion and intellectual power. Since some kind of balance will be required, opinion will inevitably enter into the striking of such balance. Burdened with that admitted subjectivity, certain guidelines, certain bounds not to be overstepped, may be suggested as a means of provoking thought as to where the balance should be and how attained.

First and foremost, the university must not compromise its integrity. That is its most prized possession. Integrity sustains its claim to a role as social critic, to an outreach function, to a mediating capacity, to the public sharing of its competence, to entitlement to teach youth, and to do research. It is also the most potent of weapons against the state or any other outside group in case of controversy. The university cannot afford to undermine the public's view of it as the objective searcher after truth. University professors of medicine, education, home economics, social work, nursing, and business could surely work directly in the ghettos and on ghetto problems without jeopardizing this principle. The same cannot be said for working abroad for the CIA under cover until exposed by independent sources of information. Integrity does not inhere in the problem but in the methods by which the problem is attacked; therefore, integrity does not dictate that kind of "neutrality" which really takes sides with the status quo.

Second, the university must maintain a distinction between corporate and individual views and acts. The institution is both a corporation and a collection of persons. For individual administrators, professors, and students, the university can and should vigorously defend their freedom, both on and off campus, in customary ways so far as these can be made to apply. For relief from the strain and overextension which comes from action-centered rather than thought-centered activities of "university persons" or from public-policy, decision-making involvement rather than classroom discussion, the academic community knows no way but negotiation, consideration of alternatives, appeal to mutually acceptable principles, and hoped-for agreement.

50

If and when individuals choose to take the law into their own hands, they will have to be left to its mercies. The university cannot be a sanctuary against the law. Indeed, institutional adherence to the law might be listed as a separate guideline. It is a boundary whose perimeters, particularly on the distinction between dissent and civil disobedience, have been cogently explicated recently by Chief Justice-Designate Abe Fortas, the solicitor general of the United States, and the president of the American Bar Association, with essential agreement.

As a corporation, the university should eschew corporate positions on public policy except where its own educational interests are involved. It should otherwise neither have nor take any corporate stance simply for the sake of changing public policy. This restraint is wise because the university cannot commit, and should not coerce, its individual members.

The university as a corporate body should make clear that it vigorously defends the freedom of inquiry which must be accorded to the members of the academic community and also the full exercise of that freedom, but that the institution dissociates itself from the content of such expressions and actions.

Third, the university must be free to do whatever it takes to keep relevant in its age. This legitimizes the outward thrust which may cause external reprisal. Feedback from the action line is a clue to relevance. In an age of rapid change, involvement is an essential laboratory for the behavioral sciences; and direct participation may be the best way to lock professors and students onto what is relevant in their age. Despite our marvels of communication, our social environment is filled with cultures, subcultures, and varying life styles totally foreign to both professors and students unless the ivory tower is left behind. Instructional, research, and extension programs which bring the university into better congruence with the critical problems of life are changes the university should welcome and risks the public must endure. Furthermore, this kind of relevance gives the universities grassroots where none existed before and in place of many now being torn up.

Fourth, the university must not lose its identity. It is fitted for some things and not for others. It *is* some things and not others. It has contemporary competitors unknown a few years ago—the knowledge industry, think tanks, private corporate contractors for both education and public services, and professional bodies with educational missions. Therefore the university will have to work out a new division of labor; but that is not to say its function will shrink. The mix will be different. Selection of options will have to be made, but probably among more options. The university cannot be all things to all people; therefore, it has to decide what things it wants to be to what people. The preservation of identity means choices but not a withdrawal from the world. It means commitment where it counts and where the need and the university's competence can be fitted together. This leaves plenty of room for innovation. While institutional identity must indeed be preserved, the admonition is not to retrench but to reassess, to establish certainty, clarity, and manageability.

Fifth, the university must not lose its critical capacity. It cannot become beholden. It cannot let itself be used. It cannot be an uncritical instrument for someone else's good. It can be a servant but not a slave. It can even become the agent of the government for particular, mutually agreeable purposes, but it should preserve the autonomy of shared responsibility in this particular and sacrifice none of its freedom of criticism in all other relations with the same cooperator. Obviously it can be seduced by its sources of income, but this is again, within wide and crucial limits, a matter of remedy by determination and forceful assertion. The desire to effect change cannot be sustained on any basis short of the exercise of the critical competence which inheres in the specialists and the custodians of knowledge who make up the faculty.

Sixth, the university must not seek power—intellectual power, the power of knowledge, yes; but not legal power or the capacity to coerce. That is the weapon of the state, of those who govern. The university may influence, advise, consult, aid in policy-making, serve as either agent or critic of government, and, above all, seek understanding; but when it seeks power itself, it abandons its claim to immunity from power. It should aspire to be on tap but not on top. Furthermore, to twist Lord Acton's phrase, power corrupts and academic power corrupts academically.

Finally, the university must not deny its accountability. It may be self-governing and self-regenerating, but it is self-deceiving if it denies that it owes its existence to society, with ultimate accountability to some representation of interests broader than the strictly academic. The university, like the citizen, is not a completely free agent. It is suspended between freedom and control, through that accountability which suits its peculiar social mission. Such accountability may run to the state, or it may run to a self-perpetuating private corporation, probably both through "trustees," the ones who literally hold a trust.

The strings may not be felt, the reins may be loose; but they are always there—as vague as "the demands of the age" or as explicit as a dictator's edict. The degree of activism and direct social and political involvement which will be tolerated cannot be assessed without the university's realization that there must be an ultimate bearing of the burden of defense if accountability presses the question. If the public is not to intrude into the university, what is the university's reciprocal obligation? What merits the restraint? Here again is the tightening tension. The challenge is to contain it, and to direct it constructively.

If these guidelines seem imprecise and unsatisfying, that in itself is a commentary on the current nature of university activism. It has moved from helping farmers with crops, teaching courses off campus, and doing what the government wants under contract to challenging established social and economic values, asserting moral positions, reordering human relations, and, in some extremes, seeking power and using physical force. It has moved from areas of consensus to areas of controversy. It has moved from operation under public policy to action to reshape public policy, from subordination to super-ordination. The extremes in such human conflict are easy to rule out, but striking the balance in the middle is indeed a tribulation. The guidelines here suggested are standards for judgment, like reasonableness as a standard of law. They are imprecise because of the subject with which they deal. Yet the line between "the permissible and the forbidden" is "reasonably clear," to use the words of Justice Fortas. "Procedure," he goes on to say, "is the bone struture of a democratic society, and the quality of procedural standards which meet general acceptance—the quality of what is tolerable and permissible and acceptable conduct—determines the durability of the society and the survival possibilities of freedom within the society." In these troubled matters, there is no escape from judgment, accommodation, and responsibility: the most ancient of rules for two men who aspire to stand on the same ground without violence. So, despite some of the current campus excesses, it is premature to despair. Someone has said that hope is at least as reasonable as despair. In fact, within bounds, progress can be wrung out of conflict. Creative tension can be harnessed to educational objectives.

As John Stuart Mill said a century ago, with some unintended corroboration of the activist thesis today, observation is also a way to truth, along with reasoning. Furthermore, he said, education is fresh "to those who come to it with a fresh mind." If looking aggressively for activism, the university community might well combine this freshness of mind with the ceaseless public promotion of the idea that the free university is indispensable and that, if restrained, it would be immeasurably less useful even to those who seek the restraint. In a sense, this is the overriding activist role the university should unhesitatingly embrace: it should busy itself in so relating to, and so serving, the public—through understanding rather than power—that a majority will concede the essential conditions of such service. In this role, the university trustees have the special task of vindicating their special trust—serving as a buffer and interpreter between the university and the public. Under these conditions, one would hope to see, as a stablizing but adaptive influence in an agitated age, the collaboration of a responsible but responsive university and a tolerant society. It takes both.

PRECIS

In considering what the policy relating to social change should be, we must first get some historical perspective. We may note immediately that the problem centers on issues which at the time are controversial. What is controversial at one period of history is not controversial at another. In retrospect, therefore, actions that were the subject of heated controversy at the time became constructive contributions when viewed from a later time.

The policy toward academic freedom should be one of complete support including the adoption of the usual procedures for hearing cases that may be in dispute. The policy of freedom should be to provide freedom to all individuals and to groups of individuals within the institution to speak, to write, and to act in relation to social action providing that they make it as clear as they can that they are expressing the views of themselves or their particular group rather than speaking for the institution.

When the institution as such takes a position, as it occasionally should, this should be the result of a consensus of opinion. It is essential to have a mechanism by which the views of individuals and minority groups can become the subject of serious consideration.

Many presidents and deans are unnecessarily timid about taking clear cut positions on controversial social issues. Seemingly they become overwhelmed by the problems of the day and lose sight of the long-term goals of higher education. They in effect become the captain of a smooth sailing ship rather than the leader of an expedition into the realms of knowledge, both stable and controversial.

The progressive, creative institution attracts interest and wins friends and fresh support.

COLLEGES AND UNIVERSITIES AS AGENTS OF SOCIAL CHANGE: GOALS AND CONFLICTS

ALGO D. HENDERSON
RESEARCH EDUCATOR
CENTER FOR RESEARCH AND DEVELOPMENT
IN HIGHER EDUCATION
UNIVERSITY OF CALIFORNIA, BERKELEY

*C*olleges and universities are by their nature agents of social change. They may, however, be activist or exercise varying degrees of restraint on action. This is a position paper on this issue. I shall deal especially with internal matters including policy formation, organizing to secure consensus on goals, and some administrative skills for dealing with conflict.

Policy formation

In considering what the policy relating to social change should be, we must first get some historical perspective. We may note immediately that the problem centers on issues which at the time are controversial. That colleges and universities are agents of social change on a host of noncontroversial fronts is well known. A prime example was the initiation of the colleges of agriculture and mechanical arts. It was clear from the beginning that the purpose of this system of new programs was to transform agriculture and provide further momentum for the industrial revolution. As another example, the medical schools, following the Flexner study in 1910, ceased to be appendages of the medical profession and became centers of leavening influence and health leadership throughout the profession. Illustrations such as the two just given could be mul-

57

tiplied, but no one questions the role of the college and university in these types of social change.

What is controversial at one period of history is not controversial at another. In retrospect, therefore, actions that were the subject of heated controversy at the time became constructive contributions when viewed from a later time.

The controversies over religion are a prime example. The theory of evolution, barely a century old, was attacked unmercifully when first introduced into the curriculum. The theory sharply contradicted the accepted beliefs of men. Although the Scopes Monkey Trial occurred so recently that it still is within our memory, the apprehensions about the new theory have almost completely disappeared. Indeed, a move to revert to the teaching of a century ago would probably meet with a storm of disapproval.

When human slavery existed in the United States, certain colleges took courageous positions that slavery was a social evil and should be abolished. We still have racism with us, but we do not have slavery. In the light of the fast moving shifts in attitude toward the problem of the Negro in the United States, if slavery were still an issue, it would be unthinkable today for the colleges and universities to stand silently by.

Reflecting further upon the black-white issue, I am reminded of an informative article that appeared in *Ebony* about 15 years ago. It described the predicaments of the presidents of leading Negro colleges and universities. Quite apart from their personal views about the Negro problem in American society, they were locked in the vise of regulations imposed by their governing boards, most of the members of which were white. I wonder whether this helps to account for the authoritarianism of the typical Negro college president—for he depends for his tenure of office upon executing the will of the board. It may help explain the attitudes of Black Power students toward "the establishment."

Of course, the social press existed for both white and Negro colleges. I recall a conversation with the president of a college operated by the Friends Society in the South. I asked how it happened that this Quaker college did not admit any Negro students—this was shortly before the 1954 court decision. He said that the board prevented him from doing so. The case would seem to be one where the board sacrificed the principles of the college in order to conform to the mores of the community. This is not a very pretty picture. It is encouraging that the Board of Trustees of Dillard University, a Negro university, is now searching for a new president among whose qualifications should be his potential for social leadership.

Let me describe an additional case on another social issue. About 40 years ago, Dr. William Leiserson, an experienced arbitrator in the labor relations field and a professor of economics at Antioch College, was appointed by the Governor of Ohio as chairman of a commission to study unemployment insurance. Antioch at this time had vulnerability on two fronts: its endowment was less than $200,000 and so it had to depend heavily on annual contributions; and under its work-study program, large numbers of students were being placed among the businesses and industries of the Miami Valley of Ohio.

The college received an avalanche of demands that the professor be fired, some of them accompanied by threats to boycott the student placement. After consultations between administrators and faculty, a consensus was reached that the professor should be supported.

Some time later, after the president of the college had become chairman of the Tennessee Valley Authority, then labeled as a socialistic adventure, the president of one of the largest manufacturing companies in the Miami Valley and a former member of the Board of Trustees of the college wrote to me demanding a change in the policy of social action. To reinforce his arguments, he said that Horace Mann, the first president of the college, would "turn over in his grave" if he knew what was happening at the institution. I took delight in reciting to the writer a number of the radical positions on such things as religious beliefs, slavery, and the education of women that had been taken by Mann when he was president of the college.

An instance of Horace Mann's courage was demonstrated when he, being a Unitarian, but president of a then church-related college of another denomination, was persuaded to join the latter church. On the occasion when his new membership was announced to the congregation, Mann rose in his place, said that he had reservations about the doctrines of the church, and proceeded to recite them. This incident was still being discussed by the villagers a half century later.

As for the unemployment insurance, needless-to-say a law was enacted by the State of Ohio, and within two decades the concept became almost universally accepted.

We can get additional perspective by considering student activism in the light of historical events. *Daedalus,* winter, 1968, published a symposium based upon the papers given at a Conference on Students in Politics held in San Juan, Puerto Rico, March 27 - April 1, 1967. Much of the discussion was an assessment of student activism. In his summary of the discussions, Professor Seymour M. Lipset states the following:

> Students were a key element in the revolutions of 1848 in Germany and Austria, and student activism stimulated the "Professors Parliament" which almost succeeded in toppling several monarchs. In Czarist Russia, students spearheaded various revolutionary movements, and the university campus was a major center of revolutionary activity. In the East European countries, where education was limited to a small proportion of the population, students were often the carriers of modern ideas of liberty, socialism, industrialization, and equality of opportunity. The important role of students in the movements for national independence in the developing areas also goes back a half century or more. In Imperial China, students were crucial to the Imperial effort at modernization, but at the same time spread republican and radical ideas throughout the society. Students helped overthrow the dynasty in 1911, and were thereafter one of the elements continually pushing China toward modernization and radical ideologies. In other Asian and African countries, students were often a central element in anti-colonial struggles.

Not all of the student-fomented revolutions have been good as, for example, their participation in the Nazi movement in Germany where they were caught up in the tide of nationalistic fervor. But generally speaking, the movements that they have joined have been constructive, at least that seemed to be the consensus of this conference.

The student activists who press for reforms today have some worthwhile things to say to us. On the subject of educational change, they are pointing out the deficiencies in the multiversity and the need again to personalize the experiences of the students. They are telling us that our value system is warped and that this warping is to some extent due to the persistent identification of liberal education with Western culture. They are saying that not only does this ignore several other great cultures of the world but also that the indoctrination in Western culture leads to certain evil consequences—emphasis upon materialism, white supremacy and the glorification of war, and tolerance of great disparities between affluence and poverty.

In respect to needed social change, they point to the enormous problems of the urban ghettos, to the influence on politics by the large corporations, and to the growing influence on government by the military. Their demonstrations against the Vietnam War have helped to influence the American public to make a major shift in viewpoint.

They identify the administration of the universities with the establishment and I think rightly so because the administration is at its top the executive arm of the governing board, and governing boards typically are populated by older persons of wealth and business and professional standing. And, of course, their objection to Mickey Mouse student governments is understandable. I do not mean to endorse the methods of disruption being used by militant groups, but I feel that much of what they are saying should be listened to and ways sought to involve them in finding solutions to the problems.

As John K. Galbraith has recently said, whenever either government or industry wants anything really important to be done, they call upon the universities to loan their faculty. Obviously this occurred in the case of the development of atomic energy; and in the light of our topic, such activities of the universities as that of managing for the government its

61

atomic laboratories is interesting. The reference to Galbraith, an economist, reminds us of the extent to which Keynsian economic theory as applied to governmental operations has replaced the supply and demand theories that characterized the century and a half preceding the Great Depression.

Perhaps the colleges and universities have never officially adopted macroeconomics as a dogma for the institution to follow. I shall presently argue against permitting any ideology to dominate a college or university. But the fact remains that departments of economics universally have adopted a new theory and the related statistical techniques. Business and financial leaders still shudder at some of the implications of the theory, but presidents of the United States have repeatedly appointed professors who subscribe to it as chairman of their economic advisors.

It would be difficult to argue other than that society has gained tremendously from the scholarly theories that have been carried from the professors' laboratories into applications in government, industry, and the professions.

Perhaps I should get down to a more specific case of institutional activism. When Antioch College was being reorganized in the 1920's, it had the dual problem of launching an innovative educational program, described in its catalog as "revolutionary," and of reforming the environment of the institution in order to lessen the constricting forces that would bear upon it. The environment was distinctly provincial and reactionary. The aim was to create an environment that would be permissive of critical inquiry and encouraging to progressive action. The aim to reform the larger community was deliberately undertaken. Here only brief reference can be made to the numerous steps that were taken on such fronts as the political, the cultural, the economic, and the health.

The local political machine was ousted from control of the village by mobilizing public support behind the dean of the college who was elected mayor. The cultural activities were the usual ones; but special effort was made to involve community members as well as college students and faculty in music, art, and drama. Some small industries were started, at first largely for the purpose of training students under the work-study program. Later certain fruits of research done at the college were plowed into these and additional enterprises. At first the industries were sponsored and owned entirely by the college. The two largest ones were originally started in a small barn and in the basement of the science building, respectively. But after a number of years of development, they were set up as separate corporations and the majority stock interest sold to the employees and to persons in the community. As a result, the community has enjoyed full employment and currently some $25 million of annual income.

Among other moves were the elimination of the segregating rope at the local theatre, forcing a reform of the electric power rates, and transforming the medical services in the community. Some of these things took three decades to accomplish. The changes in the community on almost every front have been enormous. Incidental dividends of the actions by the college have been an influx of other small industries and an immigration of intelligent and socially minded people.

Although my viewpoint toward policy formation and administrative backing for it should be clear by this time, let me summarize it briefly. The policy toward academic freedom should be one of complete support including the adoption of the usual procedures for hearing cases that may be in dispute. The policy of freedom should be to provide freedom to all individuals and to groups of individuals within the institution to speak, write, and act in relation to social action providing that they make it as clear as they can that they are expressing the views of themselves or their particular group rather than speaking for the institution.

When the institution as such takes a position on social issues as it occasionally should, this should be the result of a consensus of opinion. This is because the position taken by the institution should be that of the majority of the persons and the groups that form the institution. If this were not the rule, the college would be pushed into speaking with the voice of a minority. Also it is the total group that must bear the

63

risks. In order to avoid friction on this point, it is essential to have a mechanism by which the views of individuals and minority groups can become the subject of serious consideration and consensus of feelings by the total organization.

The folk culture and the super culture

The problems arising out of controversy are best understood if we fully appreciate the nature of the conflict. Kenneth Boulding has said that the tensions between the community and the institution develop because, although the institution grows out of the folk culture, by its very nature it becomes a super culture. Dr. Boulding is on the program and hence available to explain the technical points, but I want to discuss the subject a bit.

Colleges and universities are initiated to meet the needs of the folk culture. Again using historical perspective, we can see the reasoning of church groups and governmental units in the setting up of colleges and universities to supply religious leaders, teachers, professional services, and research findings. An elementary case may perhaps best explain this mode of origin. Suomi College in the Upper Penninsula of Michigan was founded in the twentieth century by migrants from Finland who desired to accomplish a number of things: to preserve elements of Finnish culture, to give their particular church continuity, especially through providing educated ministers, and to assure their children an opportunity to assimilate American culture. The point of greatest relevance is that the community set up an agency for the purpose of gradually evolving a new culture, blending with it elements of the old. The history of Suomi is also the history of many other colleges. If all situations were as simple as this, there probably would be no conflict.

However, it is the nature of a college or university to become a super culture. The goal is to seek truth, not to perpetuate the status quo. It would, therefore, be inconsistent with the purposes of the college to indoctrinate with dogma, including the prevailing customs and conventions. The university comes to have a high responsibility to society not only to educate its youth, which as John Dewey pointed out means change and growth, but to disseminate the ideas and methodology that are the product of scholarly and research activity. The university's responsibility is determined in part by the implementation of public policy but also in part by the individual responsibilities felt by forward looking faculty.

Thus a college or university cannot permit itself to be overwhelmed by the folk culture. It must grow into a super culture. But neither should it wrap the cloak of academic respectability around itself and withdraw behind the ivy walls. The basic problem is how to reconcile the two cultures sufficiently to have a viable situation. Conflicts there will be, and there is no way to avoid them. The question is whether the institution will submerge itself in the folk culture, thus attempting to be safe and secure, or whether it will venture to fulfill its larger responsibility in spite of the conflict.

In this connection, I should like to make a number of points. One is that an institution becomes dynamic in relation to its policies respecting social change. Reed College, for example, was founded for the distinct purpose of supplying a cultural stimulation to the Portland area. The greatness of the University of Wisconsin arose from its development of the concept that the campus of the university was the state. Thus it made the welfare of the state a principal concern. Its founding of the Legislative Reference Bureau through which to endeavor to get better legislation and better wording of laws in the state is an example. I suggest that, in both the Reed and Wisconsin cases, the high quality of intellectual effort done by faculty and students was in part the stimulation from this feeling of mission. The concept of mission was articulated by the educational leaders, but it also permeated the institution as a whole.

Secondly, educational leaders that have become historically significant figures are those who have provided fresh vision for their institutions related either to educational innovation or social advance. Those who merely navigate a safe course are doomed to obscurity. These respective courses of action mark the difference between leadership and management.

Third, the quality of the creative work by faculty and students is considerably enhanced by an involvement in significant issues, social, scientific, or other.

Fourth, the professional reputation of the individual and of the institution depends upon the publication of scholarly interpretations and findings. The purpose of publishing should be to have an impact on the development of society and not merely to count in promotion in rank or salary increases.

As indicated earlier, I make a distinction between critical inquiry into controversial issues and, in contrast, the adoption of an ideology. The inhibiting effect in Soviet Russia of having adopted dogmas relating to economics and to genetics has been clear to the scholars of the world and, more recently, to the Russians themselves. Scholarly efforts should be free. The institution should not impose any "ism" upon its faculty and students. The college needs to move with care and consensus when it adopts an institutional position and must preserve the freedom to dissent. I may add that this applies equally to radical new ideas and to the preservation of the status quo. All too often we do impose, through church controls, board resolutions, or presidential decrees, the beliefs and conventions of the folk culture.

I should like to add a thought on a very sensitive matter. The ecumenical spirit that prevails now among the three branches of Western religion hopefully will spread among all of the religions of the world. The people of the world must agree upon values and goals for mankind if we are to live together in peace. College youth are beginning seriously to question many of our most sacredly held values. These values should be examined afresh, and the basis for doing so should be the experiences of cultures round the world. My point is, then, that within our colleges and universities we must apply the test of dogma versus critical inquiry to religious beliefs as well as in other areas.

Organization to gain consensus on goals

If a policy is pursued that supports academic freedom and also freedom of speech and action in the larger sense that I have been describing, it will be important to organize in a manner to reduce tensions and conflict to the minimum and to determine when institutional activism is warranted.

For this purpose, the test of a good organization is one that will assure sufficient intercommunication among the parties of interest to obtain reasonable consensus about goals and a willingness to incur the risks. This means participation in decision-making respecting policies and programs. In my judgment, the dangers from these risks usually do not materialize; and if they do, they do not remain for long. The institution that makes constructive contributions toward social change will attract fresh support.

Colleges and universities today almost uniformly use the bureaucratic model of organization. The final decision-making power rests in the highest executive, subject to confirmations by the governing board. Communication is primarily downward in the form of directives. This is, of course, the legal structure, and I think it is unrealistic and undesirable to do away with the corporation as the central organizational structure. Certain adjustments within the structure can, however, be made. One is to secure as members of the governing board persons who are more representative of the diversity of cultural, scientific, civic, and ethnic interests of the community and also persons who are representative of the academic interests. This, to put it baldly, would mean breaking the domination of the business-oriented interests that now compose our boards.

Another adjustment lies in the realm of behavior. Institutions do not need to behave as though the authority were autocratic. Indeed, such behavior is not in tune with the academic goals, since a university is composed of professional men and women who are peers. For this purpose, a distinction can be made between policy and program formation in the determination of which there should be widespread representation and on the other hand the implementation of policy and program which requires a certain job-pyramided administrative structure.

Another form of organization being advocated by some SDS students and AFT faculty would be to recognize administration, students, and faculty as discrete groups, each with its own interests and organization. Representatives of these groups then would negotiate agreements for the operation of the institution. I recognize that organized labor has had degrees of success in presenting its positions to management in this manner. In some instances the SDS and the AFT have succeeded in obtaining concessions from the administration. I shall dismiss this alternative somewhat abruptly, however, because I think it is antithetical to the essential nature of the institution. A college is a goal-seeking organization, and there needs to be a consensus among administration and faculty, and also students, concerning the goals. The effort of the institution being intellectual, the organization needs to aspire to the highest level of excellence in student achievement and research findings. The process of negotiation and mediation tends to arrive at compromises that are at the lowest common denominator. Such armslength bargaining may produce better working conditions for the faculty or studying conditions for the students, but it will not elevate the general tone and quality of the institution.

There is a third alternative with special reference to the function of policy-program formation. Rensis Likert calls this the group participative form. Its characteristic is an involvement in decision-making. Its implication for a college is that in policy-program formation the top administrator functions in the role of educational leader. As such he is a member of a circle rather than the director. Within the circle at the top level are representatives of administration, of faculty, and of students. In my opinion these representatives should be freely elected by the respective groups with only the president and the top academic officer being ex officio members. The faculty as the professional group should have the largest number of representatives, but the representation of all groups should be sufficient to provide a feeling of genuine participation. I assume the need to have a series of levels for decision-making and that at each level there would be similar circles that were representative of the primary interest groups.

If the administrator sits at the table with the other representatives to provide leadership and, subject to the occasional need to use his legal authority, joins in the decision, he will be in a much stronger position within the institution and be able to perform a superior service exterior to it. He will have been forced within the meeting to analyze the proposed action in a manner to gain mutuality of understanding, and this leads to confidence. Because of his understanding of the faculty-student points of view and his own commitment within the group, he will be speaking to his board and to the public not just for himself but as spokesman for the institution. This is a highly important point because it has to do with his effectiveness in action and also his control over his own nervous tensions.

Group participative theory thus requires a reorganization of the membership of the board of trustees and of the policy-program forming councils within the institution. With this changed composition, the intercommunication should be greatly facilitated. Some presidents follow the policy of keeping board members far removed from the ongoing work of the institution. They do this with good intentions, namely to keep the board from interfering with the academic program. This policy may have worked at times in the past; but in the present day of newspaper and TV communication, this seems an unwise policy. Incidents occur on the campus that shock the board members. They are pressured by telephone and mail to clamp down on the institution. They get defensive and resent it. They have no understanding with which to be persuasive in explaining the actions of the institution.

If the personnel of the board cannot be reorganized, ways can be found to increase the communication between the academic group and the board. In my former role as president, I persuaded the board to reduce their attention to the physical problems of the campus in favor of meetings for an exchange of views with representatives of the faculty and sometimes of the student body. Ordinarily these were preplanned occasions with official groups from within the institution preparing a discussion to present to the board with a follow-up interchange. No action was taken, but a spirit of fellowship was fostered and a degree of mutuality of understanding and of confidence ensued. I am certain that it placed the board members individually and as a group in better position to represent the institution in places where funds needed to be secured or the public needed to be better informed about the institution.

A final word about organization. Today both faculty and students demand larger participation in decision-making. I think both groups can make constructive contributions. Whether or not one agrees with this point of view, it may nevertheless pay to find orderly means of bringing them in on consultations because if the process is not an orderly one, it will occur as confrontations. I do not mean that disruptions and confrontations can be entirely eliminated. But the following of the militant groups can be reduced if the general run of students and faculty feel that they have genuine representation in decision-making bodies, and if there is feedback to them.

Administrative skills in implementing policy relating to social action

Administrative finesse in dealing with cases of tension and conflict probably comes with the acquisition of experience. I would not pretend to be able to tell you "how to do it." I will, however, state a few principles relating to administrative attitude and action which may commend themselves.

Two successful university presidents have described their techniques in books on administration. Harold Dodd stated that the wise administrator will do a large amount of conferring with his colleagues before making decisions or implementing action. Henry Wriston told how he would informally drop into offices throughout the campus. He made a habit of doing this before reading his morning mail, which suggests the relative importance he placed upon communicating with his professional colleagues as distinguished from becoming a slave to the mail and the telephone. I would commend both procedures, but would add that it is very important to keep in constant communication with the representatives of responsible groups. It is they who have the ability to bring pressure upon the administration, and hence it is they who need most to understand the considerations that the administrator can bring to their attention. Furthermore, in this situation communication is more freely given because the individual, in speaking for the group, communicates more freely than if he were merely voicing an opinion of his own.

Part of the objective is to get feedback concerning administrative actions and administrative image. An administrator needs to be conscious of the image that he gives. Let me describe an example. Sometime ago I had occasion to discuss with a bearded student activist the qualifications of the president of the university in which he was a student. Because there had been some student-administration tensions on this campus, I described the professional qualifications this president had which I thought made him a leader of high potentiality. I referred to his grounding in the fundamentals of organization, his understanding of social psychology, and his known ability to communicate with people. I said that, given an adequate exchange of views and some time to permit organized bodies to take action, this president would provide the opportunity for achieving many of the ends being sought by the student activists. The answer of the student was very brief, "That is not the image that comes across." It seemed to the students that his communicative efforts were confined to issuing directives of the usual authoritarian type.

Jumping to another point, when an administration or an institution becomes the subject of attack, it is important to endeavor to counter with peer influence. It reminds me that, in a recent case when a university president was asked by a militant group to prevent the Dow Chemical Company interviewers from coming onto the campus, he responded quietly, "OK, if the students want it that way, let's abandon employer interviews. It's a costly and time-consuming activity for the university to help with student job placement, so why do it if the students don't want it." This seemed to me to shift the issue back to the students and to provide the opportunity for a larger student voice to be heard. The advantage to the administrator in having an organization to assist him in determining policy is that he has organized support for his position. The presumption is that the organization represents the majority view on the campus. If this view is questioned, the matter can be reassessed.

When helping to conduct the study that led to the establishment of the State University of New York and other reforms in the state, Owen D. Young, chairman of the commission, taught me a good technique. Invariably he would put an opposition leader in a key position of responsibility, trusting that an examination of the issue and of the facts would soften or win him. This worked beautifully in several crucial situations. Note, however, the importance of confronting the objector with the necessity of examining the pros and cons of the issue.

Adequacy of communication is so much the key to all resolutions of conflict that it is important to realize that true communication diminishes as the conflict intensifies. According to the social psychologists, conflict occurs when differences about goals arise. As the views about goals widen, communication lessens. The lessening of communication causes the parties to intensify their disparate views. This in turn reduces effective communication still further. Thus a downward spiral of conflict is set in motion. The problem is to reverse the spiral, and the method of reversing it is to increase the intercommunication about goals.

An administrator needs to work on his skills of communication. He needs to be articulate about the role of the college or university. When problems exist he needs to be able to examine them fully and communicate all facets to interested parties. This practice is the opposite of secrecy about problems.

I should like to say a word about administrative leadership. Many presidents and deans are unnecessarily timid about taking clear-cut positions on controversial social issues. Seemingly they become overwhelmed by the problems of the day and lose sight of the long-term goals of higher education. They in effect become the captain of a smooth sailing ship rather than the leader of an expedition into the realms of knowledge, both stable and controversial. An institution that functions smoothly may grow in size but it will probably remain static and may decline in quality. Timidity breeds mediocrity. Faculty and students gain confidence in a leader who grasps fully his role of leadership.

I think this applies also to governing boards. Trustees admire an imaginative spokesman for the institution. They respect a man who has sufficient strength to combat them on their own grounds and, because of superior knowledge about the nature of the problem involved, wins their approval and support. Furthermore, as already said, the progressive, creative institution attracts interest, and wins friends and fresh support.

SELECTED REFERENCES

Henderson, Algo D. (Ed.) *Higher education in tomorrow's world.* Ann Arbor, Michigan: The University of Michigan, 1968. 189 pp.
University educators from 14 countries analyze the goals of higher education with special reference to the role of universities in social change.

Henderson, Algo D. and Hall, Dorothy. *Antioch college, its design for liberal education.* New York: Harper, 1946. 280 pp.
An analysis of the policies, program, and mode of operation of Antioch College, an institution that has been active in influencing social change.

Likert, Rensis. *New patterns of management.* New York: McGraw-Hill, 1961. 288 pp.
Discussion of participative forms of organization.

Lipset, Seymour M. *et al.* Students and politics. *Daedalus,* winter 1968. 344 pp.
Essays describing the activism of students and historically evaluating the results of student militancy in various countries of the world.

PRECIS

Education is an "industry" which is a significant sector of the economy. It is now a little larger than agriculture as a proportion of the gross national product and the prospects are for its continued growth. In spite of this, if one contrasts the number of agricultural economists with the number of educational economists, the disproportion of the effort is a beautiful testimony to social lag.

As one looks into the future one sees the university as an institution of increasing importance in society, with great resilience and staying power, but also as an institution in some degree of continual crisis. Part of this is a matter of sheer growth. The kind of decision-making processes which are appropriate in small institutions are not appropriate in large, and the sheer lag of organization in universities tends to give them growth trauma. Part of this is conservation of tradition and the fact that most faculties, especially, see little reason for doing anything today that they did not do yesterday. Which is the simplest decision-making rule even if it is not always successful.

Certainly if the universities do not adapt themselves to the modern world they will very rapidly run into new institutions which will provide them with stiff competition, which is good at least from the point of view of society.

THE UNIVERSITY AS AN ECONOMIC
AND SOCIAL UNIT

KENNETH E. BOULDING

PROFESSOR OF ECONOMICS

UNIVERSITY OF COLORADO

$\mathcal{E}$conomists have been surprisingly tardy in recognizing that education is an "industry" which is a significant sector of the economy. It is now a little larger than agriculture as a proportion of the gross national product and the prospects are for its continued growth, partly because the sheer growth of the total stock of knowledge means that a larger proportion of real resources must be devoted to transmitting knowledge from one generation to the next and partly because, being an unprogressive industry technologically, its relative price keeps rising, like haircuts. In spite of this, if one contrasts the number of agricultural economists with the number of educational economists, the disproportion of the effort is a beautiful testimony to social lag.

There is no generic name for a unit of economic organization. The word "firm" is usually restricted to profit-making organizations. There is no general word for nonprofit or what might be called "not very profit-making" organizations such as universities, schools, hospitals, municipalities, and so on. Surprisingly little attention has been paid to this sector of the economy even though it is growing very rapidly. Still less is there any general term for a unit of organization considered as an organizational behavior unit in the total network of social relationships.

In economics there is a quite elaborate theory of the firm based on the assumption of profit maximization. There is no corresponding theory of the nonprofit organization, even though this occupies very much the same kind of position as the firm in the total social system. The only nonprofit organization which has received much attention from economists is the household or the family spending unit, but the problems involved in large-scale nonprofit organizations (NPO) are quite different and cry for attention. The university may be taken as typical of this important class of organizations.

A look at balance sheets

A good many elements in the theory of the firm can be applied directly to the NPO. In the first place, any organization has something like a balance sheet in the form of a position statement or state description of it at a moment of time. A physical balance sheet or general position statement consists of a simple list of physical assets and liabilities. These include, on the asset side, cash, debts due, accounts receivable, inventories, buildings, land, and certain intangible but extremely important items which might be called reputation, good will, or morale, representing the capacity of the organization for continuing to function as an organization. On the liability side we would have such things as accounts and other debts payable, and perhaps some items of negative good will representing disadvantageous personal relationships, personnel, traditions, or reputations.

In making a state description, the role of the existing personnel is of great importance. We need to distinguish between the role *structure* on the one hand, which consists of all the clearly recognizable positions in the organization, and the role *occupants* on the other. The role occupants may either under fulfill or over fulfill the role and hence may contribute positively or negatively to the good will items in the balance sheet.

In some cases, such as professors with tenure, the role occupants have a considerable degree of contractual permanency. In other cases, there may be a high turnover. In either case, an accurate state description would have to involve some kind of estimate of the value of the various role occupants to the institution on the asset side, and some account of the obligations of the institution to the role occupants on the liability side.

An essential element in the state description is the inputs into and outputs out of the institution for some accounting period. An income account also has to include items of depreciation of the existing assets or conditions, such as the running down of buildings or equipment or (strictly) the decline in skills and reputation of the faculty members.

The dynamics of an organization are closely related to its inputs, outputs, and depreciations. Its processes may be divided fairly sharply into those which are subject to what I have called the "bathtub theorem" in which the relation of inputs, outputs, and stock is that of simple addition and subtraction. An input adds to the stock and an output subtracts from it, so that the net increase in the stock in any period is equal to the input minus the output, just like water running into and out of the bathtub. An excess of input over output raises the stock by exactly that amount. An excess of output over input lowers the stock similarly.

This principle applies in exact form, for instance, to cash balances. The increase in a cash balance in a period is exactly equal to the difference between what has been paid into it and what has been paid out of it. In the case of other physical assets, again, the bathtub theorem applies if the increase in the stock of any particular asset is equal to the input minus the output. The output in this case, however, may include depreciation as a form of consumption. Input may be either production or purchase; output may be either consumption or sale.

When we come to the more subtle assets and liabilities involving reputation and good will, the relations between inputs, outputs, and stock may be much more complex than the simple additive relationship. These might be called the informational variables. Here, even though there are clearly functional relationships between inputs, outputs, and stock, these relationships may be very complicated and not follow simple principles of addition or subtraction. Thus, in the case of an individual, an increase in his knowledge is not simply the result of an excess of input of information over its output. Information is not conserved as money stocks, and, as to a considerable degree, the physical capital are conserved.

The university is particularly subject to this principle because one of its major activities is teaching, which is a prize example of nonconservation. When the teacher teaches a successful class, the class knows more and so does he. There is no sense in which teaching results in a loss of information in the mind of the teacher and a corresponding gain in the mind of the student. Everybody gains together. Good will or benevolence and the closely related concepts of morale and reputation are also nonconserving quantities. A "good" administrator creates good will among the faculty which in turn makes it easier for him to be a good administrator. An abrasive person by contrast can easily create cumulative ill will and declining morale and reputation.

One of the problems of all organizations, profit-making as well as nonprofit, is that accounting systems are designed primarily for those inputs and outputs which are subject to the law of conservation and are not adapted at all to deal with those elements in the organization which involve information and which do not obey the law of conservation. As a result, all organizations tend to operate with a perverted information system, with good information about certain aspects of the organization and very poor information about other aspects which may be equally important from the point of view of the organization's success or survival.

This means that, while there is a clearly defined ritual in financial accounting, the all-important informational accounts are never made explicit and one has to rely on the good sense and almost on a kind of unconscious skill on the part of administrators and others in keeping the nonfinancial accounts in good shape.

A "good administrator" is precisely the man who is sensitive to the total state or condition of the institution. Therefore, he does not sacrifice the nonfinancial aspects to pettifogging detail or accounting formalisms. Nor does he neglect the necessity for making financial accounts balance and for keeping the institution continually capable of meeting its financial obligations.

The fuzziness of nonfinancial accounts introduces a bias into the decision-making process. This is a problem even in profit-making organizations where, even though the financial accounts contain a large part of the measure of the success of the organization, the nonfinancial aspects of the institution frequently determine its financial success or failure. Under these circumstances, a decision-maker in almost any organization is like a man with a telescope attached to one eye and a frosted glass over the other. He might be able to see something very well, but he would certainly not have binocular vision.

Any theory of the organization, whether profit or nonprofit, must have some sort of abstract view of the process of decision-making. In the elementary theory of the firm, information is supposed to be virtually perfect and costless and the decision-making process is simply based on profit maximization, that is, the firm is supposed to select those inputs and outputs at which the profit is at a maximum. In the case of the nonprofit organization, this view is clearly inadequate from the start. Nevertheless, it is not easy to find a substitute for the maximization principle. We can, of course, restore the maximization principle formally for all organizations by supposing that what is maximized is utility. All this really means, however, is that everybody does what he thinks is best at the time, which can hardly be denied but is a principle that does not necessarily have a great deal of content.

Maximization theory, however, does have one virtue. It implies that all decision-making processes involve some kind of evaluation of the changes which are believed to result from a decision. The weakness of maximization theory is that it has prevented the development of a taxonomy of decisions simply because it assumes implicitly that all decisions are alike. This may not be so. In a university, for instance, decisions about appointments and promotions may be made on very different principles from decisions about curriculum, about fees, about recognition of student organizations, or about the building of dormitories. The list could be extended almost indefinitely.

Furthermore, the decision-making process always has to be studied in the light of its organizational setting. The authoritative legitimator of a decision in an organization may not correspond at all, for instance, to the "real" slot or level from which decisions actually emerge.

The structure of authority

Every organization has a certain written or unwritten constitution which represents the generally accepted structure of authority. The points of authority may be a single role such as department chairman or dean; they may consist of a committee which has to make a collective decision; or they may consist of certain veto powers. No matter what the written constitution, every organization tends to have an informal constitution consisting of the people who control channels of communication or who are influential with the authoritative decision-makers.

The larger the organization, the more important this informal constitution is likely to be, simply because the formal lines of communication lead to a progressive impoverishment of the information flows to the higher executives. A hierarchy is a set of wastebaskets designed to sift out what each member of the hierarchy regards as the essential information which will go up to the next level. It may well be that the information which is really wanted at the top is sitting in the wastebasket somewhere in the seventh level of the hierarchy.

If large organizations are to operate successfully, they must develop a good deal of redundancy and informal communication. These informal redundancies are often very hard to identify. Nevertheless, "knowing" the organization becomes one of the principal avenues of advancement in the hierarchy, and this consists essentially of a sensitivity to who it is that really makes the decisions. These informal organizations are apt to be particularly important where the occupants of roles which are high in the hierarchy are incapable of handling the information overload which is always the penalty for authority. Under these circumstances, the supposedly powerful members of the organization tend to rely on cronies and informal communications which may not be part of the formal organization network at all.

One sees this principle operating most clearly in political organizations where the upper members of the hierarchy do not "rise" through the hierarchy but are imposed on it from without, as for instance, the President of the United States. In universities and also in corporations, where promotion at least in the middle levels of the hierarchy is often made from within, there tends to develop an "official family" within the administration who have a strong subculture among themselves and lively communications among themselves but not very good communication with the rest of the organization, either informally or formally.

This situation can often cause a great deal of trouble as decisions are made in the light of increasingly imaginary images of what the situation is like. There is an iron law of hierarchy, that hierarchy in itself tends to corrupt communication because there is always inadequate feedback between superiors and subordinates, but also a man gets promoted to the hierarchy by pleasing his superiors. This is a skill which may make for euphoria but not necessarily for survival. It also leads to a progressive elimination, as people rise in the hierarchy, of the kind of capacity which is needed at the top where there are no superiors to please. This is perhaps why, in universities and in many other organizations, presidents and even deans are frequently brought in from outside.

Maintenance decisions and growth decisions

A real taxonomy of decision is beyond the scope of this paper, but it may perhaps start with the fundamental distinction between what might be called maintenance decisions and creative or growth decisions.

81

Maintenance decisions, as the name implies, are designed to maintain the institution as an open system. The Office of Admissions, the search for replacement of faculty and administrators, and the bulk of financial decisions fall into this category. The larger, the older, the more respectable the organization, the more likely it is to confine itself largely to maintenance decisions. The danger here is that maintenance may not be adapted to a changing environment, and an institution which neglects the creative decision may find itself at a sharp competitive disadvantage in rapidly changing environments.

Even in universities, it is very hard to get recognition for the really creative decision-maker. He is often somebody who stands outside the regular respectable channels of academic and institutional life. This is the sort of man who opens up a new field, who creates a new department, or a new institute, or a new kind of activity such as extension, new fields of teaching, and so on. The long-run success of an institution, and this is especially true of universities, depends in no small measure on the ability to tolerate and even to encourage people of this kind. Here again, the capacity of an institution to recognize the intangible accounts is often the key to its success.

The problem of location

A very interesting problem in the theory of the university which has not been very much studied is the problem of location. A university which is too isolated will find it hard to maintain a constant input of stimulating visitors and also the circulation of its faculty among other institutions and assignments. On the other hand, an institution which is too close to the center of things may find it hard to maintain its inner integrity because it is too distracted by easy access. This is perhaps why Washington has not produced a major university in this country and why one is almost tempted to describe the ideal situation for a major university as 30 miles from a major airport. These, however, are speculations without much evidence.

Especially at the level of second and third rank institutions, the random element is often very important. There are large numbers of people, for instance, who are capable of what might be called "maintenance operations" in the role of the president of a university. There are very few people who are capable of a creative operation in this role, and for any particular institution it is largely a matter of luck whether they get a maintenance man or a creative man. Two creative presidents in a row and the university is either ruined or advanced into a higher rank. Like the selection of presidents of the United States, however, the process of selection of university presidents has a very strong random element in it.

The problem of financial survival

The problem of financial survival of the university is closely related to its function as an economic unit in society. The financial survival of any institution depends on its capacity to maintain an input of cash adequate to cover its cash outflow. In growing institutions the input of cash should be slightly larger than its outflow to allow for growth in the total stock of liquid assets. An input of cash, however, corresponds to an output of something else and an outflow of cash to an input of something else.

It is usually fairly clear what the outflow of cash creates in the way of inputs of something else, for the outflow of cash is, for the most part, paid out in exchange for something. It purchases inputs in the way of supplies, equipment, buildings, and the services of faculty and employees. The input of cash, however, is derived only in part from the exchange system, for instance, from student fees, medical fees, hospital charges, royalties, and payments for contract research. A large part of the cash input of any university is in what is called the "grants economy" and is derived either from appropriations from legislatures, either state or federal, which are in turn derived from the tax power, or they are derived from endowments, alumni contributions, private gifts, or foundation grants, all of which represent one-way transfers.

The economic position of a university is very deeply involved in the total grants economy, and up to now we have not had very much study about this or theory about it. We can perhaps stretch the economist's concept of exchange and suppose that grants are made in response to some "product." The product in this case, however, is not a physical or exchangeable product, but it is a state of mind of those who have the power to make grants. Just what it is, however, that produces a willingness to make grants on the part of those who make them is often quite mysterious. I suspect that the best theory of the foundation is that it is a 90 percent random process. I am not sure that government is much better. One of the problems here is that the willingness to make grants is often quite unrelated to the performance of the grant-recipient. By contrast, one of the nice things about the exchange economy is that the institution which produces a saleable commodity has at least some control over what it produces, and hence its own decisions may affect its cash input. In the case of a grant-recipient, the grant often strikes, or does not strike, as the case may be, like lightning—the risk, however, being much less insurable.

A factor in the university situation which is receiving increasing attention today is a very remarkable change in the nature of the market for university services. This has two aspects—the increase in the proportion of income derived from research as opposed to teaching and the increase in the proportion of income which is derived from the federal government by contrast with either state or local government, private endowments or fees. There has been a shift also in the relative support which is given to different sections of the university. In the last 25 years, for instance, there has been a great increase in support of the natural sciences and of the medically related sciences. We are now seeing a similar rise in support of the social sciences, while the support of the humanities lags.

These changes in the market environment inevitably have profound impacts on the condition and on the decision-making processes of the whole institution. There is quite a strong case for a certain amount of viewing with alarm. How much alarm is appropriate is not easy to say. It is particularly hard to evaluate this change in the financial environment from the point of view of its impact on the intangibles, such things as loyalty to particular institutions, the willingness to perform roles which are not directly rewarded, and the relative role of the university itself, and outside sources of funds.

Anxiety is at least being expressed that this change in the market environment is corrupting the integrity of the university as an institution. It is feared that the tradition, which goes back to the Middle Ages, of the university as an academic community with widely shared responsibility among the faculty for its decision-making and a corresponding identification of the faculty with the institution itself and with its welfare, is giving way to the notion of the university as a convenient source of status, a kind of launching pad from which appeals can be made for outside funds.

It can be argued that we should simply accept this phenomenon and adapt ourselves to it. What is significant is the total republic of the intellect, not any particular embodiment of this in a local university. In American universities, especially, the very political structure of the university as a corporation, usually governed by a self-perpetuating oligarchy or occasionally by an elected body of regents or trustees, has tended to undermine the notion of faculty responsibility for the particular university and its governance. The American university has been described as a benevolent tyranny checked and balanced by an active labor market, and while this is a caricature the face is recognizable. The active labor market, however, has one unfortunate consequence. It creates a pretty sharp distinction within the university itself between the visible "cosmos" who participate in the active labor market and who are, therefore, largely independent of the particular institution which they condescend to grace with their presences and the "locals" who are less visible and who do all the work around the house. It is not surprising that, under these circumstances, severe internal strains may appear.

The status of students

In these days one cannot allow one of the strands in the composition of the university to go unnoticed, that is, the students. Although there are times these days when one gets almost a little nostalgic for apathy, certainly this is a very remarkable student generation raised as it has been from babyhood on Dr. Spock and TV. The great problem here is that students occupy an uneasy status within the university. They are not merely customers, although they do have somewhat the relationship to the organization that customers have to Sears Roebuck. Neither are they quite *members* of the community, though they are perhaps closer to this these days than to being mere customers. It is this intermediate status between the customer and the member which makes the problem of student unrest and dissatisfaction so hard to handle.

Universities are reluctant to admit students to full membership in the community with decision-making rights simply because it is felt that they are not around long enough. They do not have sufficient responsibility for the long-run future. A university which would be parallel to a consumer's cooperative in which the students are not only members but the owners and the ultimate governing authority would be conceivable. This could almost be called the "Legend of Bologna." Up to now at any rate this form of organization has not even gotten off the ground. Nobody really knows whether it could survive.

One does not have to go to this extreme, however, to recognize that there is increasing pressure these days for the recognition of students as members rather than as customers, and the universities have to respond to this in some way. One possibility is elected student representatives on the Board of Governors. Certainly what has passed for student government in the past is proving increasingly incapable of carrying the weight of the new demands.

It has become apparent this year also that, as legal and judicial organizations, universities leave very much to be desired. This aspect of the university has functioned in the past partly because it has not been seriously challenged. When it is challenged, the universities find they have no repertoire to fall back on. In matters of student discipline there is no "graduated deterrence"—nothing between the slap on the wrist of admonition or probation and the blockbuster of suspension or expulsion. Perhaps universities are going to have to set up small jails under the heading perhaps of meditation chambers to provide suitably graduated deterrence for suitably graduated assaults. The disturbances of the last few years raise very acutely the question of the judicial status of the university within the framework of the larger society. Is the campus part of the city it is in, or is it not? The medieval tradition of the university as a sanctuary still remains but is perhaps becoming increasingly impractical.

A look at the future

As one looks into the future one sees the university as an institution of increasing importance in society, with great resilience and staying power, but also as an institution in some degree of continual crisis. Part of this is a matter of sheer growth. The kind of decision-making processes which are appropriate in small institutions are not appropriate in large, and the sheer lag of organization in universities tends to give them growth trauma. Part of this is conservation of tradition and the fact that most faculties, especially, see little reason for doing anything today that they did not do yesterday, which after all is the simplest decision-making rule even if it is not always successful.

A very interesting question is whether universities increasingly are going to run into competition with other types of teaching and learning institutions. Corporations, for instance, are increasingly taking on functions of teaching, learning, and research which previously were regarded as somewhat the preserve of the university. Certainly if the universities do not adapt themselves to the modern world they will very rapidly run into new institutions which will provide them with stiff competition, which is good at least from the point of view of society. This is perhaps the most optimistic note on which to end.

INTRODUCTION

The Wednesday Night Colloquium became known as that simply because it took place on a Wednesday night during the progress of the institute. Professor T. R. McConnell chaired the discussion and participating were three of the institute faculty and three guests. They agreed in advance to pay special heed to the topic of the institute which is the title of this book, but their personal interests and broad backgrounds brought a great diversity of viewpoints to that topic. The colloquium itself provides a study of the several schools of thought within higher education which are struggling to redefine its role in society. For that reason a transcription of the colloquium was considered to be a fitting way to conclude this collection of papers.

The institute faculty members participating were: Eldon Johnson, Algo Henderson, and Kenneth Boulding. The three guests were: Sir Peter Venebles, vice-chancellor of the University of Aston, Birmingham, England; Robert Ross, national director of the activist New University Conference and a faculty member at the University of Chicago; and Richard H. Peairs, associate secretary of the American Association of University Professors and director of its Western Regional Office.

WEDNESDAY NIGHT COLLOQUIUM

T. R. McCONNELL, CHAIRMAN

I'm not going to summarize the issues that have been discussed at this conference. The assumption is that there has been a great deal of continuity to this conference, that you know what the main issues are, or you know which issues have been carefully avoided by the speakers. So we don't need a summary of events today.

Now let me proceed to very quick introductions without any biographical information. Sir Peter Venebles is the vice-chancellor of the University of Aston in Birmingham. As I am sure you all know, the vice-chancellor corresponds, in our institutions, with the president of the university. Eldon Johnson of the University of Illinois, who spoke this morning; Algo Henderson, of the Center for Research and Development, Higher Education, who spoke yesterday; Robert Ross, the national director of the New University Conference, with offices in Chicago; Kenneth Boulding, who is to speak tomorrow morning. He is the program director of the Institute of Behavioral Sciences at the University of Colorado; and finally, Richard H. Peairs, associate secretary of the Association of University Professors and director of the Western Regional Office of that association. Sir Peter has agreed to start off with a brief statement of some of his reactions to the issues that have arisen in this conference.

Sir Peter:

Ladies and gentlemen, I may say the agreement was a required volunteer activity. But I accept it with great pleasure because it gives me an opportunity, on behalf of my wife and myself, to express our thanks for being invited to this conference which we've found most stimulating. We'd like to say how thankful we are to everyone who has been so kind and welcoming.

I shall need that before I've finished because I am asked, in this very brief statement, which is five minutes, to deal with the whole British aspect of higher education. I know that there is a slight difference between our two countries, but I assure you that this can't be done in five minutes. I shall very quickly say, in relation to the issue of this conference, what the general British position is at the moment. Then I shall go on to pick out four things which seem to me to warrant further consideration.

The British comparisons are very much the same as here. We have the same issues — there is no need for a new theological doctrine of the geographical distribution of original sin. . . all of it in America, and not Great Britain. We have the same issues. We have students too. We vary in size of the commitments. The intensity varies, and we haven't yet got to some of the intensities which you are unhappily experiencing. Nevertheless, we have our incidents which have been quite sizeable. I have, personally, survived two sits in or sit ins, and it was never part of my ambition to have downtrodden students. But such was the case.

One thing I hope we shan't get, which I deplored in the beginning of this conference, is the general implication that if one is activist, if one is wanting a very radical point of view, one is courageous, one has *the truth*. Whereas those who hold the pluralist view, and support the multivariant university, are lacking in courage, discernment, or truth. I've found this singularly unfortunate. I hope you won't mind my saying so, and I wish the speaker had been here for me to say it in his presence.

The degree of activism which we have is a variable and is considerable. But so far, apart from sits in and the occasional pot of paint, it has followed fairly consitutional means. But the issues are important. The issues include participation of students in the work and life of the university. The representation or membership of students on senate and council or faculties and departments is now actively under discussion. In some cases, definite moves are being made. I think the general atmosphere of universities, as a whole, is much more forthcoming in these respects than it has been in recent years.

One of the issues is the conduct of examinations and curricula. Another one, the important one, is disciplinary procedures, and here we have a particular circumstance you may not know about. We have a committee, called the Laity Committee. Mr. Justice Laity is the chairman, considering at what age young people should become adult. This committee has recommended, and the government has accepted, that the age be lowered from 21 to 18. So that every student would have come to the university as an adult, and this clearly has very considerable implications.

Of the four things that I would like to consider, first of all, I'd like to deal with the development of the social sciences in Great Britain. They are developing very fast. It's gently come in upon our notice that the community at large is the laboratory of the social sciences. We are faced with similar issues which have been raised in this conference, but it would be a general view that there is a very proper purpose and place for the university to be investigating and establishing facts, but much more important, the theoretical foundations of growth and change.

To go on to what we would call the development. Science and engineering in the university are largely being concerned with the theoretical basis; development is taking place outside in the analogy. For the social sciences, the university should be that kind of place in which the work of other agencies is supported, fostered, and the general atmosphere is in their favor.

I am a member of the National Council of Civil Liberties. I've been for many, many years. But it's inconceivable, and this leads to may second point, that I would be asking the university or making a statement on behalf of the university, on behalf, or in support of, the National Council of Civil Liberties.

So then I come to my second point — statements by chancellor and university, institutionally, in a corporate sense. I think I'm right in saying that the British view would be very close to that of Chancellor Heyns. I'd like to elaborate that, but to save time, I think that's the simplest definition. I think there's, perhaps, more leeway in the chancellor on certain things, making his personal position known. But I think it would be generally accepted that he must, as argued by Chancellor Heyns, be very careful of the reputation and well-being of the university.

My third one is one which has not been mentioned at all, but to a Britisher is very striking indeed. Clearly, in any high issue of well-being of the university, it's of the greatest importance that lay people, the lay members of the governing body, and the academics should be close together. The very strong contrast between the American and British systems (we've found it before, but I've never realized it in full until I came to this conference) is that in your system, you have these separated. In British universities, the Executive Council is composed of lay people and academics. On my own council of about 30 people, there are about 13, 12 or 13, academics — voting full members, alongside the lay people, and all these issues are discussed within the executive body, not at variance elsewhere.

I could give various other consequences of this. I have been through a whole series of evolutions. From a college of which I was the principal, I attended the governing body like your regents and as a nonvoting member, made my case. They made the judgement. I transmitted it back. Then it became a college of advanced technology in which five of us became members of the governing body and the position was altered. When we became a university, the proportion was very markedly increased. I can assure you that the dialogue between lay and academics in that situation is most fruitful.

My last one is to make a comment on academic standards and the involvement of students. I think there is much more inclination now, in the rich universities, to bring students into discussion on academic curricula and the like. But it would be my judgement that there would be a resistant point — a very firm resistance, on involving them in the conduct and judgement of examination results. And I would regard that, in academic circles in Great Britain, as the sticky point. Consultation as much as you like, but professional judgements are for the professionals. I hope that gives as succinct account as possible in the time.

T. R. McConnell:

Thank you, Sir Peter. We'll turn next to Robert Ross.

Robert Ross:

I also would like to thank WICHE for inviting me and all of you for being so very cordial. This meeting has been a revelation to me. In listening to your discussions, I find that a lot of one's preconceptions are true, and a lot are false.

Let me lay out a very schematic and, I hope, not too discontinuous criticism of the way I feel the conference has gone about its discussion. Perhaps it was the way you must go about the discussion, so then it's not a criticism but a suggestion for what I would think needs to be thought about over and above the general level of issues that have been on your mind.

My impression is, from many, many places, that what the rebels that you all face demand of you is not so much that you take corporate positions on the war, but that, in many places and it obviously varies, you live up to the neutrality and detachment which you think that you have. I tried to say this earlier in the conference, and I don't think that point was communicated well. Let me take a moment to do that.

But first, a digression. When you talk about the university as an agent of social change or whether it should be, I find it

93

very perplexing to discuss that unless the society that's doing the social changing is at least referred to, the nature of that which is changing, and how it is changing, and the things that are moving it to change. These can't eternally remain kind of a vague thing out there. I think you'll agree that that has not been discussed at the meeting.

Now, what is it that is being demanded besides the taking of corporate positions? Not only the students, but increasingly younger faculty members who aren't attempting to organize, in political ways, see that the university is a very active agent — perhaps not of change — perhaps of maintenance of the society as we see it and as it is obviously developing.

In a society — and now we must refer to the nature of that society — in a society which is a capitalist system, power flows in certain predictable and routine ways. Money has a great deal to do with the kind of service you can get from any institution. I think that if you as executives would look at your labor relation centers, business schools, and so on, that proposition would stand up, that, in fact, the center of gravity of service, intellectual, physical and concrete, that you render to society, is serviced to the privileged sectors of that society. Serviced to those who need it the least but can pay the most for it. And finally, serviced to those most interested in maintaining it in all its good but also all its bad ways.

That isn't neutral. You just can't maintain that proposition. There are more polemic, and to me more important, ways in which you are not neutral (or your institutions) and I don't mean to make a personal attack at all. Many of your institutions, not many numerically, certainly — and this again, I tried to say earlier — have been very important cogs in the machinery that created the weaponry and the technological base for the cold war and the arms race. Just as importantly to me as a social scientist, your institutions have been a very important place for making the cold war and anticommunism a respectable myth and a respectable religion in the United States of America. This is not the executives' fault at all. I would just as willingly make the indictment of the last 20 years of scholarship in the social sciences.

I would argue to you that we are reaping what we institutionally have sown, that the war in Vietnam is not a temporary aberration but, in fact, has to do with that flow of events that the institutions represented here have been crucial to. Indispensability does not necessarily render power. That was one of Marx's errors. Nevertheless, indispensability does, to the one who is indispensable, render a moral obligation.

Your obligation is not necessarily to say the war is evil, but to do what institutionally you claim to want to do, to be more detached from those forces. For example, again something I mentioned, are you going to treat draft resistors for going to jail — and they are going to jail — with the same solicitude that you treat returning veterans? Are you going to assure that the resources, the research, etc., that are available to the city planner of Oakland, be available to the Black Panthers?

I do not indict you for not being concerned most recently with the poor and black people but for the way in which that concern has been expressed. Because you're all budget minded, and your faculties are budget minded, and money in this country buys service, the money which the Economic Opportunity Act and HUD and HEW have freed for socially concerned action research has flowed in ways which are not oppositional. I don't say you have an obligation — I would like you to agree with me that an oppositional style in the society is good. You don't have an obligation to act if you don't agree with that, but don't claim that you're neutral unless you have that balance. You have all mentioned balance, but I don't see that balance in your institutions. I see, as I said, the center of gravity of your influence, to be of service to those who are trying to keep the lid on the pot.

Another thing that is disturbing to me, as an intellectual, is the disdain and contempt (condescension is a polite word that was used earlier in the day) that I find in your attitudes—disdain and contempt for the feelings of moral outrage that the students presently have. It seems to me that the argument, as it has developed thus far, is that in extremity, like Nazi Germany, in extremity, you all are for changing your present orientation. What happens if you believe war crimes are being committed now? What happens then? If you believe that the extremity is here, it is not thousands of miles away, and it is not somebody else, but your own people who are the criminals.

T. R. McConnell:

We offered Kenneth Boulding a special dispensation since he hasn't heard the discussion of the last two days. The special dispensation was that he could wait until everybody else had spoken. But if he's moved at the moment, I will withdraw the dispensation and say it's your turn.

Kenneth Boulding:

I must confess, as an old Methodist, I'm a bit convinced of sin by Bob. I think he's said some very acute and very uncomfortable things. I think it is true that the universities are a part of society. It is true also that the powerful have power. The only trouble is, after you've made that discovery, what do you do about it? And this is not always easy to say. It is one of the things that I don't understand very well, speaking even as a social scientist.

What are the processes in society by which power is shifted around? It does shift, and this is one of the most fundamental changes in society. There are shifts in the power structure. I have an opinion that it usually happens quite accidentally. I have a feeling that no society is exempt from this proposition. After all, this isn't just a property of capitalism.

It's hard to see much difference, from this point of view, between capitalist and socialist societies. As a matter of fact, in socialist societies power is even more concentrated. At least there's a little balance of power here. In our society the House of Lords is represented by the Rockefellers and DuPonts, the House of Commons, shall we say, is represented by Congress, and the church is represented by the university. Thus, we do have a pluralistic society. I'm in favor of checks and balances — especially when the balance is what I can write checks against.

The universities cannot help but be agents of social change, whether they want to or not. They are agents of change in the total sphere of knowledge because it is knowledge which is the prime agent of social change. But of course, social change may be blind, and it very frequently is. We do things around the university, we know not what we do. We certainly do not know what the consequences are. Very often we couldn't care less. We do have some very interesting examples of this, Dr. McConnell, in your paper. It is certainly the way the natural scientists and the biological scientists horse around without any notion of the consequences of their behavior. It is very striking in this regard that universities are enormous agencies of social change. But a good deal of this is blind, in the sense that . . . we aren't aware of it.

The social sciences are supposed to be the eyes and ears of universities in regard to the impact on society, but I'm afraid we don't have 20-20 vision. The real point is that our knowledge of social dynamics is still very primitive. Under these circumstances, almost anything we do will have opposite consequences from what we intend. That goes for the radicals and revolutionaries as well as it goes for conservatives . . . almost everybody. It is because we are operating in a system that we don't understand very well.

Finally, a point which Dr. McConnell seems to me to have implied in his paper, that the hardest things to get at are the sins of omission. It's easy enough to spot the sins of commission because they're committed. We would have you spot what isn't there. This is the hardest thing to do, and I think we have to think a great deal about it.

The involvement with the Defense Department wouldn't be quite so bad if universities had established a few peace research institutes, would it? But they haven't. I've been trying to raise money for peace research for 15 years. I've just given it up. You can't raise any money for this. You see, the idea that you should apply human intelligence for the problem of peace is laughable around a university. Nobody gives it a minute's thought. It's perfectly all right to apply human intelligence to destroying people. That's quite acceptable. I think the sense of moral outrage, among those who have moral outrage, is about five percent. I feel a great deal of this myself.

On the other hand, moral outrage can easily go off into quite unprofitable movements. We had a session at our home with some of our young radical friends a few weeks ago which went long after midnight. One of them said to my wife in a tone of utter disbelief, "You really believe in sociology, don't you?" With a sense of absolute astonishment, you see. Maybe she does; maybe I do. She may be right in believing in economics at times.

I do believe in the intellectual task. It's still very much in process and this is something that the universities must never forget. Their prime objective is the intellectual task. This doesn't exclude other tasks. I'd hate to see a university composed of people who have no sense of moral outrage just as I would hate to see my daughter marry an economics man. On the other hand, the major task must be kept in mind, and this is a task without which moral outrage will be spilled on the ground. We saw a very good example of this in the Prohibition. And I must say an awful lot of my radical friends remind me of Prohibitionists. That was the last great grass roots program of moral outrage that we had in this country, the last grass roots movement. It was disastrous because it was moral outrage unilluminated by very much knowledge of social systems.

T. R. McConnell:

Richard Peairs, will you now contribute to the discussion?

Richard Peairs:

In so far as I can express the viewpoints of the AAUP, I will spend a few moments stating the obvious. Then I will be quiet and listen to the rest of the discussion because I'm curious to see where it leads. The association's views on these matters are familiar to each of you knowledgeable in the statements of policy which have long been a part of the doctrine of AAUP. They are statements of the principle of responsible practice in the profession for which the association is guardian.

I am, of course, referring first to the 1940 statement of principles and academic freedom and tenure. It is not in that statement that one finds support for or against positions espoused either by Mr. Wofford or Chancellor Heyns. But when Committee A, in its semiannual meetings, discusses the implications of the 1940 statement with reference to an instant case at Institution X involving Professor Y, it becomes quite clear that the position of the association is that academic freedom flourishes when professors have opinions, but institutions do not.

Therefore, I would assume that Committee A would support the view of Chancellor Heyns that the institution which maintains the broadest spectrum of academic freedom is that institution which permits the widest exchange of views on its campus without itself adopting an opinion. We do have what is sometimes called the loophole or the escape clause of the flexible interpretation of academic freedom as it can be generated at an institution with relationship to a special interest. The church-related institution which has been developed by a special subcommittee is instructive, I think, in this area. And I would commend it to your study.

The association is concerned more deeply than it ever has been before with reference to the concept of shared responsibility in the government of institutions of higher learning. The statement developed by the association, jointly formulated with the American Council of Education and the Association of Governing Boards of Universities and Colleges, is coming to have great meaning. We are endeavoring to seek added interpretations of this statement to give guidance to faculties, administrations, and boards of control.

I think one of the most astounding aspects of present unrest on campus, to me personally, is the amount of power which students have ascribed to faculty members. They themselves (the faculty) have not recognized at this point that they are possessors of such an immense amount of power.

Shortly after the dinner hour, I went to my car to pull out some materials from the file, because I thought it might be useful for you to hear two phrases from two handbooks of institutions of higher learning. They are mostly instructive, I suppose, for the students and perhaps for those of you who are interested in this very challenging process of the affirmation of responsible standards of practice in a faculty handbook for all of the constituencies of your institution.

There is one handbook for an institution in the West that says this about on-the-job conduct for members of the faculty: "You are to render full, efficient, industrious service in the performance of assigned duties. If insufficient work is assigned to fully occupy an employee at any given time, he is expected to notify his supervisor so additional work can be assigned." For those of you who are members of student bodies, that's an extract from a faculty handbook from a degree-granting institution which is accredited in the western United States.

There is another relatively well-known state institution that has, in a faculty handbook, which was published, or republished in October, 1967, the following language under the section entitled "Resignations and Terminations for Cause": "Regardless of the provisions of 1, 2, and 3 above, (this is where some notice is taken of tenure) a faculty member who commits a serious offense affecting the public interest may be terminated summarily by the president."

This is not 1905; this is 1968 that we're talking about. We must recognize that, while some of the flamboyance of student protest captures much attention of the higher education community, there still are patient and plodding and perhaps generally unromantic activities which are being directed toward the improvement of conditions of life for all members of the constituency of higher education . . . faculty, administration, and perhaps even boards of control.

We are intimately involved in a new endeavor associated with the rights and freedoms of students, a statement about which some of you have heard which has now been endorsed by the annual meeting of the association. It is a jointly formulated document and one in which all of the formulators agreed at the beginning to take no independent action with reference to interpretation or enforcement. Considerable efforts are being devoted toward the establishment of an appropriate vehicle for the wider promulgation and announcement of this statement to the profession and its appropriate enforcement.

Enforcement, of course, in the pattern of association response, always takes the form of persuasion. Some people may see this as a form of power. We prefer the gentler phrase.

With reference to the association's position on the patterns of disruptive behavior, I think our position is clear. It's been acknowledged from the *New York Times* to the *San Francisco Chronicle*. This is not necessarily both ends of a single spectrum, but at least a rather clear acknowledgement by a broad section of the public media. It is the insistence that faculty members particularly look carefully at their own institutions and seek to develop processes and procedures to protect the institution from disruption. This has been the expected position and the position which has been reiterated over the last 14 months by the association.

T. R. McConnell:

Thank you. I don't want to put a gloss on the remarks made by members of the panel, but I take it the last speaker suggests that, before we change the world abroad we might change our own institutions, in certain regards, and that we might be more effective in promoting social change if we make some changes in our institutions.

Eldon Johnson:

I'm reminded, from having heard Chancellor Heyns on an earlier occasion, that part of our problem arises out of a lack of agreement about what the university is. I think as we've carried on our discussion, much of the time we're not sure who the university is—faculty, students, trustees, what have you—or what the nature of the university is.

I'd like to raise a question about our agreement as to what the university's responsibility is. What would be your reaction to a flatfooted statement that the university's responsibility does not extend to the making of public policy? If we had agreement on that, we'd be down the road a good way. I don't know if anybody would challenge that or not.

T. R. McConnell:

Say it again.

Eldon Johnson:

That the university does not have the responsibility for making public policy.

T. R. McConnell:

Anybody respond to this?

Kenneth Boulding:

It depends a little on what you mean by this. There's a difference between what you may call formal authoritative decision-making which is clearly not in the hands of the government or of the university but which is in the hands of duly constituted authorities, whoever they may be. But then there is also the problem of how decisions are actually made which is another matter altogether.

I have a feeling that in all organizations the only real decisions that are made are at about the level of a second lieutenant. I mean, this is the instructor — something like this. That is, by the time you get up the hierarchy there really are hardly any decisions to make. I don't need to be President of the United States to make one special decision in four years. A president of a university is lucky if he does that. That is because the channels of organization, the channels of communication, and the decisions get pre-empted in a way.

In this sense, the university is a very powerful agency for making social policy. This is the difference in influence and power that we have. I would say this is something that you always have to bear in mind, a real responsibility. In the sense that the university muffs it, society is much worse off. The university has a moral responsibility toward society, I would say, in the total process by which social policies are made.

Eldon Johnson:

May I react to that? You're saying, I believe, that public policy-making is a process. It has a certain continuity. This

102

leaves us with the crucial question "Where along that line does the university get off?" You're saying at one extreme, that part of this — and this is where I put the knot in — part of this conception of public policy-making is pre-empted by and assigned by society to the machinery of government. The formal part. The making of statutes and so forth. That's not the university's business. You would accept the knot there.

But you're saying that somewhere leading up to that — at least advising with some input with regard to public policy — this is appropriate for the university. I think this helps some in clarification. I think we are prone to be absolutist in our discussion here in that we say we start down a road we never can leave. It seems to me that we don't have to go to the end.

If you're talking about the university making a study of something, beyond the study phase comes, perhaps, an advocacy phase or a political power phase, or the use of public office phase, then the making of public policy. And someplace before you get to that end, the university gets off. It can get off way back at just having made the study it wants to and having offered some consultative advice.

T. R. McConnell:

Where do you think it ought to get off?

Eldon Johnson:

I think it depends upon the particular issue. I think we get off at different places with respect to different questions.

T. R. McConnell:

For example?

Eldon Johnson:

Well, to get into a safe field 10,000 miles away. . . .

T. R. McConnell:

I was trying to get you into an unsafe field if I could.

103

Eldon Johnson:

I was once a party to an international project to make recommendations about the educational system in a small foreign country. An international team made the recommendations. It recommended the establishment of a university and reorganization of teacher training institutions, a lot with respect to primary and secondary education.

It seemed to me that we were not the university, but the university might have been in the same position, that our job was done when we made the recommendation. What was done about it with respect to public policy was clearly the job of the government of that nation.

I think this is true with much of our university relationship to social issues, but not always. In some cases I think you'd make a study and the study is action oriented. It runs from research, which is action oriented, into public policy. There's a continuum here, and you carry it on in the action phase into the ghetto, or whatever the problem is, and see it a long way down the road. This is still short of, let's say, getting mixed up with government or confusing a role with government in making new public policy.

T. R. McConnell:

Mr. Ross, do you have any comment on this? Or should we save your time for something else? Any further comment or questioning of the panel members?

Sir Peter:

I'm always a bit chary about making close comparisons. Perhaps it might help if I point out one changing part of our university scene. I don't know if it will happen over here at all. With the growth of government power over education in England — in the United Kingdom — which has been very considerable, it has been found that the case of the universities tended to go by default. If you have 17 universities as was the original number before the war, now expanded to 44, you have 44 independent, autonomous, nonrelating institutions, all relating only through a vice-chancellor's committee for purposes of consultation and sharing of practices in what's being done.

It was found that the university case with the government was going by default at the time when the other part of the university, the higher educational system directly under the government, was getting all resources by comparison and being pushed along by government, so it was thought. I give the worst fears of that time.

Now, what in practice happened was that, first of all, the universities have come together, and I would say are now entering a period of interdependent autonomous institutions, no longer acting entirely separately but acting in concert on certain matters which they regard as of great importance.

I would say, of those who started the vice-chancellor's committee, in Oxford and Cambridge Club and the rest, that it would be anathema that the vice-chancellors, collectively, should be speaking with government and to government on behalf of the university as a whole. But this is now happening. The vice-chancellor's committee now has regular meetings with the university grants committee and also with the Secretary of State and the Department of Education and Science. A very definite effort is made to influence policy at top level before decisions are made, and not to receive the decisions and then reserve the right to complain about them. I think that this is a very marked change, but it may not be possible on your scale. I think with us it's certainly come to say.

T. R. McConnell:

But this is with respect to affairs of the university, not with respect to the affairs of the society at large. Am I correct?

Sir Peter:

Yes. This is quite correct. But I was going to raise the question earlier which was raised in the discussions, as to whether the institutional representation by universities should be for education only or for the whole affairs of the nation. I think the British view would be that it could be for education, and

105

is now being done in the ways I've mentioned. For other matters it would be done by freedom of speech on behalf of academic faculty, and the university should see to it that the conditions of the university were such that that could be done.

T. R. McConnell:

Thank you. I think we'd better open this to comments and questions from the floor. If you wish to, as I said, you may address a question or a comment to any member of the panel.

Floor:

I would like to hear Mr. Ross' comments on apocalypse.

T. R. McConnell:

Mr. Ross, you're asked to speak.

Robert Ross:

The other afternoon I said and was corrected — the gentleman from the University of Redlands corrected me — that there's nothing you can do, that each of your universities would be disrupted, and he corrected me. The proper formulation should have been that there's nothing that you predictably will do that will head off these disruptions.

The original reason for these disruptions was the nature of the institutions. That is, they're doing wrong. They're going to pay. On the other hand, there are more superficial ways to analyze the problem, and I suppose that those are the ones that you are more interested in. That is to say that there is a growing mass movement. It is historically unique. I assume that you're aware of that, and if you go back to the history of even the depression radical movement, you find that, in every instance if you compare campus-by-campus chapter sizes and so on, they were much smaller and certainly less able to mobilize energies than the present student-based movements against the war, interracial justice, and so on.

Moreover, and this, for your information, is in doubt, the nature of the political theory that these movements is generating, may or may not be truly new. Recently, I've been a little depressed at what I think are echoes of the Old Left, in theory, coming out of the organizations I helped found. Let me just say that one of the reasons that these movements not only have grown to the point where they are now but also seem to me to be expanding is that they are able to tap the very basic current in American youth.

I don't know what generation gap means but I do have a great confidence in the proposition that the subcultural differences between the adolescent college culture (its more Bohemian or Hippie or political or whatever the deviant groupings might be called) and the standard American administrator's culture are really growing very rapidly. There is some sort of tremendous divergence in the realities within which supposedly part of the university community lives.

At any rate, what I was saying the other day is that there is an internal dynamic to these movements which is accelerating. In the last 18 months — obviously I shouldn't have to remind you that it's greatly accentuated but has been building for at least five years — the universities seem to me to have slowed their rate of response, if not reversed it. I think that, in a sense, some of the administrations that I know about are beginning to have the view of the counter-insurgency operation in other spheres. That is, you meet the first complication, or the first guerilla raid, with overwhelming force, thereby as a deterrent to future foolishness. I don't mean necessarily police force, but suspension, dismissals, whatever. Unfortunately, I don't think (unfortunately in your point of view, fortunately for my point of view) I don't think that that's going to work because I think that so many of the young people that you're prepared to throw out of your institutions are prepared to be thrown out, that the threat will not be successful.

The second thing is an entirely different direction. One of the students from Oregon mentioned the other day how successful the McCarthy campaign had been in drawing students out of irregular and into regular political channels. I think that that's going to backfire because McCarthy's going to get whipped by very undemocratic means, and they're going to be a bunch of very alienated young kids who don't have the advantage of being political and being sophisticated.

What's going to happen, I think, is that these will turn into the lone wolf provocateurs and saboteurs. A very small number of them. So even that last best hope for orthodoxy, I think, is going to backfire. That's what I mean. I think this is a time of great promise. Don't get me wrong. And I think it should even be a time of great promise for you. Remember how unhappy people were about the organization man decade and the silent generation and all of that? It's clear that the best students are smart now, politically smart, culturally smart, creative. This whole Hippie business, which I came along a little too late for, is creative. It has tremendous energy. It's not so terrible, but it sure is disorderly, and there's going to be more of it.

T. R. McConnell:

I was just going to suggest that we keep our minds on the question for the conference. Which is "Should the university be an agent for social change, and how?" Let's keep that in the front of the discussion. There are all kinds of things we might say about disruption and student power and so forth. Let's keep our minds on that main issue.

Floor:

You missed the point. . . .

T. R. McConnell:

Well, that's very possible.

Floor:

The university is already an agent of social change. The students are making it that way. As I have said before, the issue of choice is that you're either going to have to become repressive and keep it from becoming an agent of social change, or else you're going to have to find a way to attempt it in creating established methods to turn that social agent to change into a local institutionalized type of thing.

T. R. McConnell:

Thank you. That, I think, brings it around to the point. Perhaps.

Floor:

I wonder if someone on the panel would comment on the differences between the leadership of George Meany and that of Walter Reuther on the Trade Union movement as an institution of social change. I think there are some fruitful analogies here which bear exploration.

T. R. McConnell:

Is anybody interested in trying to bring that on to the major issue?

Kenneth Boulding:

This is the first time I've heard the word leadership applied to this phenomenon. I would say the organizations were indistinguishable.

Floor:

Do you think they are comparable?

Kenneth Boulding:

Yes. But I don't see a great deal of difference. I mean the labor movement hasn't had an idea for 30 years, not in Detroit or anywhere else.

Robert Ross:

I didn't understand the question.

Floor:

In a study between the two people, one is an administrator and the other is inclined to keep a movement alive, directing the union's attention to the larger questions of public policy, international peace, disarmament, and so on. Reuther has gone astray, obviously. Meany has not. He's minding the store. I think this deserves comment because the university is being asked to stop minding the store and to go astray from its traditional function.

Robert Ross:

Who's asking it to do that?

Floor:

I think the students are asking it. I'm not placing a value on this. I'm saying that's the subject of the conference.

T. R. McConnell:

Somebody wishes to say more?

Floor:

I wonder whether this view might also be illustrated by suggesting that the way in which the conference has proceeded has, to my way of thinking, got the reaction rather than the action. If I may suggest an action be proposed, it might have been to have begun the conference with a statement of critical social issues. Then we might have considered how the universities might have related themselves to those issues. I wonder whether the panel might react to this suggestion as an alternative — both the approach, and whether the panel does not agree that really we are reacting defensively rather than constructively.

Robert Ross:

I agree with that very much. I'm not acquainted with the general culture of the group so I don't know whether that would have been practical. With 20-20 hindsight, it seems to me that that's a reasonable way to go about getting at the issue of the university as an agent of change, it's to ask what needs changing.

My concern has been, in discussion with people privately and publicly to the extent I can, to begin with issues — the issues of war and peace, the issues of racism in the society, the issues of who the university serves as a client, how you can put the universities' services into use for those who can't now pay for them, and how the university can be an agent of redistributing power.

That's what I'm talking about. The way to begin is to talk about the society that's changing. It need not be terrible. People can learn. Do you know, for example, that many of you are going to be called tools of capitalism in the coming year, or lackeys of imperialism or some such phrase? This is very uncomplimentary and perhaps theoretically tangential to your own concerns, but I would think that that's really worth thinking about. What is it, as officers and institutions that you're officers of, that will lead your students to say that? Or some of your students.

T. R. McConnell:

Incidentally, that was said before I was 32.

Floor:

I'd like to ask Dr. Peairs this question. We have seen some conspicuous instances, Berkeley and Columbia being obvious examples, where it has seemed that students and faculty have tended to favor, to share, and to agree on a more active role for the university community as a whole — social change — and the administration has seemed to act as a brake on the way in which students and faculties have wanted to go.

In a great many other institutions, large and small, throughout this country, the situation is quite different. You have students and administrators sharing and agreeing on concerns and moving toward the university as an agent of social change, and the faculty serving quite definitely as a brake. Would you comment on those differences, whether you think that's a fair assessment, and why you think these differences exist?

T. R. McConnell:

A good question.

111

Richard Peairs:

I can comment. If you're asking, first of all, if there are differences in the community of higher education, the answer is obviously "Yes." If you're asking if I have done research on these differences, the answer is "No."

Do the differences of opinion that exist among the major constituencies of the institution — the administration, the faculty, the students, and other interest groups that are concerned — share a commonality in the position of the devil's advocate or the guy with the black hat? No, not in violations of academic freedom, not in violations of effective university government, and I am sure not in differences of opinion with reference to the proper role of the university in society. Faculties at one institution may have attitudes that are more closely akin to administration than at other institutions, but I don't know what that really means in terms of the importance of the debate we face.

To return to an earlier point, I think the thing that troubles me the most about the contemporary debate on the role of the university is the general low level of this debate. If there is a criticism that can be leveled against the quality of the product of American higher education, it's the statement generally that people want to change the university. The quality of the debate astonishes me, in the fact that it consists primarily in the exchange of slogans. When we talk about disruption as the first element in a discussion about the role of the university, I think we must have a rather sparse and spare program to suggest. I think it is quite unfortunate. I do not misread the temper as I hear it expressed.

Algo Henderson:

One of the problems of our large universities today is the manner in which the faculties subdivide themselves in the form of academic departments throughout the university. They do this partly because the rewards relate to this. That is, the rewards in the university circles go toward scholarly work, and this is commendable. I'm not suggesting it isn't. But in the meantime, they separate into little walled-off compartments, talking among themselves, but having a minimum of interchange on the larger ideas that should pervade a university.

There's almost no conversation, university-wide, on highly important issues unless some crisis comes along that forces, say, a faculty senate to have a meeting on the subject. I'm inclined to think that our universities are in a bad way in terms of organization by having permitted what one graduate dean calls "these little baronies" to build up and exist and then protect their vested interest. Some new devices need to be found to cut across these channels to develop interdisciplinary bases for work. There's quite a bit being done in research in this respect but very little in terms of teaching and almost nothing in terms of the great issues of our society.

T. R. McConnell:

Yes, again?

Floor:

Perhaps we could bridge this age gap, or generation gap, by asking that Mr. Henderson put his finger on the main issue which is that the students perceive the university as having the power to bring about changes. They haven't defined those changes, but they are disappointed in the university. They expect the university to change so that it might better perform the function which they anticipate.

Dr. Johnson:

It appears to me this illustrates our dilemma. The Vietnam War is surely a critical issue. The university ought to take a position on that in the public policy sphere, but if the politicians, whose business it is to make public policy with respect to the Vietnam War, have differences of opinion about this, we can't expect the universities, given an entirely different role in society, to know precisely what the truth is.

Floor:

If I'm hearing things for the last three days correctly, the collective view apparently is that militant students are demanding that a corporate position be taken on policy issues by the universities. I don't think that's so. You are asked to practice what you preach in terms of what your mission is. Ross touched on this. It seems to me it's the central issue.

Robert Ross:

I tried to do it twice. Keep going.

Floor:

I'm trying. The observation of my contemporaries is that we're clouding the issue of student revolts and the power reaction to this failure of the university to meet this form of requirement. Let's not any longer let the meeting be clouded with that. Let's get on with this central point about what we expect from them.

Floor:

I direct this to Dr. Johnson, primarily because he's the one who put his finger on it. In his remarks about where would you get off. Suppose you're conducting counter-insurgency research in Thailand. That research fits Chancellor Heyns's criterion for appropriate research. That criterion was: Does it have a body of content with which we traditionally deal? Probably so. It's a sort of science, and this involves other programs with which the university is engaged. The answer, there, is "Yes, probably so."

What seems to me to be missing from Chancellor Heyns's criterion is "Does it fit the moral mission of the university?" This mission is free, independent, critical inquiry. And the fact is, there is no truth on this matter, of providing free, independent, critical inquiry. Our services are being purchased for the fringe benefits that the money this kind of research renders.

That brings me to this point: You do your counter-insurgency research; you make your recommendations; and then you wash your hands of the matter — if I'm to follow Dr. Johnson's suggestions accurately. My question to you is

"What's your responsibility when that research that you have done is used in an immoral way?" Let me suggest you heed your own Dr. Boulding's remark about biologists horsing around without regard to consequences or acts. It seems to me that this is the central issue.

I am displeased with our intellectual corruption from the left. Much of it is pure and simple 1930's gall. Moreover, it's so old it's painful. And yet, even Chancellor Heyns didn't address himself to our corruption from, let me call it "the establishment." We are being asked to do research for fine reasons — nationalism, save the country, service to the public, tax support. But the question that we refuse to answer is the acceptance of that kind of life, that kind of research, with the attendant obligations that go with this, corrupting the spirit of free, critical, inquiry just as badly as the physical disruption encountered.

Let me suggest, as I did days ago, that people are going to make you pay consequences for the acceptance of that research just as Chancellor Heyns indicated they would pay consequences in the form of political retaliation if they refused to do that kind of research.

The question, it seems to me, is "What do you do with that responsibility?" You've created your research; you've made your advisory recommendations. You wash your hands, and now that research is taken up for a clearly immoral purpose.

T. R. McConnell:

Eldon Johnson, you would comment?

Eldon Johnson:

That's a good question, and I think we're dealing here, obviously, with the question of public policy, as we're dealing with a question with political overtones, and human behavior. There are no simple answers. Incidentally, that's why we have Congress. That's why we have formal political processes by which these things are decided and public positions taken.

115

On the question you raise, as I understand your case of counter-insurgency research, first of all, I doubt very many institutions would take on that kind of research.

Floor:

That kind of research in the generality sense?

Eldon Johnson:

Yes. Well there's plenty of that. And the university's gotten into plenty of it. I take it the Manhattan project must be the prime example. To develop the atomic bomb. But I - I'm not sure that we really can expect to follow all of these specialized kinds of projects, they are projects, through to all the conceivable consequences, and I think the atomic development of the atomic bomb is an example. Scientists have been perpetually perplexed about what the consequences are. Some have organized to do something about it. But I don't - I suspect it's asking too much of the physicists and the other scientists who developed this technique - for them to have explored it all of the way through to all of the public policy consequences they're after. That seems to me to be something that has to be resolved by public, political means.

Floor:

Should the individual who is a member of the university deal with these kinds of questions that have a questionable moral sense?

T. R. McConnell:

Dr. Johnson, do you want to say anything further? There's a gentleman way back there.

Floor:

I would like to propose a positive note, but the only way I can propose a positive note is to do it negatively. I was rather appalled when Professor Boulding indicated that he was un-

116

able to find any money floating around that might be available for research into the nature of peace, and what might be involved. I guess the only thing that is more appalling is the fact that the lack of that money has resulted in no research in peace. In ways of a very substantial nature, really, this has contributed constructively to the formulation of public policy. I confronted this question myself, and I had my turn at being a radical in the days of the creation of the National Student's Association.

In those days, being a radical was wanting to develop lines of communication with the International Union of Students. I went to the president of a prominent midwestern university to get the first thousand-dollar allocation for student government that that university had ever made. To do so, I had some authority that might be responsible for creating such a budget. The solution to the problem of peace that had to be found then, as I saw it, was not in terms of the capability of any academic discipline to contribute because it was rather clear that the establishment wasn't really ready for peace. They were geared up for war. The only thing that I could think of that could contribute to this was the exchange of students that might provide a little understanding in the academic community in terms of a comparative experience, and I pursued this.

I'm not hearing from the new radicals, though, any positive proposals for carrying forward the research that might serve as the basis for a more enlightened public policy. I don't hear about the young faculty members devoting their time to the formulation of research proposals that could get at the positive issues. I'll admit that it's certainly more colorful politically to oppose than to propose, but it seems to me that if this conference wanted to take a single issue that has been neglected by the university community, they should be at the heart of the university's contribution to public policy. It would be to examine the nature of peace and how this can be accomplished in today's context.

T. R. McConnell:

Any further discussion?

Floor:

You refer to the students so often with this mixture of humor and disdain that Bob Ross described as contempt. You don't know what they're thinking, and you're very anxious about it. There is a mood of anxiety in your assembly here, which is only slightly veiled by the good humor and the exchange of asides and jokes that you can make.

I think there are several reasons for this that have already been touched on. One of the reasons that there have been constructive proposals from the new left, for kinds of research in social change and peace and so forth, is that their style of operation is a style which very few university people are really trained to appreciate.

In the language of the new left, the people around the universities simply aren't keyed in. They cannot serve these people because they do not understand their language. The university function, by and large, in the old form, is to get a concrete proposal written up in a 20-page foundation grant format, obtain a grant, and then get office space and shut it off somewhere in the sociology department or in the physics department or God knows where.

Then leave it there to operate on its own and finally come forth with reports three or four years later. Meanwhile, the only contact the people working on such proposals will have with the other people, even in the university, will be at cocktail parties and such chitterchat.

It's incumbent upon you to try to understand what this style of the new left is. Some of you, I think or I hope, have gone to an SDS meeting or a slate meeting or whatever it may be.

T. R. McConnell:

Can you tell us what the style is fairly concretely and briefly?

Floor:

There's a matter of recognizing another form of democracy that's going on, for one thing. You don't necessarily begin with a proposal from a small group of intellectuals who will work, just in secret or semisecret, with the university administration. It's something that has to go on in the street. It's a matter of communicating with people in a way that universities are not requested to communicate. To see it, you have to participate in it.

Some of their language, to me, is just as disgusting as the language of many university administrators which I have heard here. It's just as artificial, awkward, and irrelevant. But to understand it, you've got to get mixed up with it.

Floor:

I face a rather serious dilemma in my own mind. I'm very sympathetic to the claims that are made for a moral position to be taken by the university. But suppose we're dealing with a faculty scholar who has a medieval personality and finds himself interested in a project dealing with counter-insurgency in Thailand. Is he, as an individual scholar, stopped from his desire to pursue this line of inquiry by consensus of his peers in the university community? Or do we grant him freedom to do so? Even though he may be misguided, poor soul. In essense, do we tell Schlessinger and Rostow to go to hell. This is what I'd like to know.

Richard Peairs:

The question probably could better be answered by Chancellor Heyns and so I will arrogate myself to answering for him. I think that one of the criteria which he proposed which was not discussed earlier by one of the respondents was the fact that the problem which exists has someone who is interested in it. This is a very essential criterion in university activity. If someone in the university is interested in a problem, this is a pretty good reason to permit him to investigate it. One of the reasons that universities have organized bureaucracies that do trouble practitioners of knowledge art is that they do have to make value judgements as to whether or not the time is available, the space is available, and the resources of the institution can permit it. But, in the abstract and the ideal situation, I think that the answer to your inquiry is "Yes."

One more comment. I think I can contribute just a little bit to an additional body of knowledge. I do not find the statements disgusting which I have heard nor do I find the rhetoric terribly confusing. One of the difficulties which we face is that there is stereotype in the behavior of both sides or all sides of the multifaceted controversy. I recall some recent research that pointed out that there were, in 1967, as many disturbances with reference to hours in the women's residence hall and prices of the food in the cafeteria as there were disturbances relating to the Vietnam War. 1968 may be a different year, but I think we have to recognize that all disturbances are not all the same and that we should be very careful in the way that we describe these activities as not putting them all in the same bag.

Floor:

I recently became a graduate student after being a faculty member. One of the first things I observed, to my dismay, was that truth is where the money is, at a university. The things that are explored are the things where the funding is available. The selection of research topics and the direction of the flow of energy in graduate study is where the funding is. The funding is from those agencies who are the clients of the university — government agencies for the most part, many of them with very, very important projects for health and education but also some projects involving the possible destruction of our our civilization.

I raised the question again and again: "Do we have an obligation as administrators to balance out the picture and to provide truth — opportunities for people to study where the money isn't?" The answer is "People don't want to study where the money isn't. It isn't fashionable; it won't lead to professional advancement; it can't be documented; there aren't enough prestigious people in the business."

So we're left with a very despairing picture as to how we might attack this. As university people and as educators, we've lost sight of some of the moral qualities that go with educational leadership and some of the philosophical duties that develop upon us as civic leaders, leaders of the republic of learning. We haven't gone to school for this. We've gone to school for our own separate disciplines.

I think we have some learning to do and some studying to do to attack the moral problems of our age. It can start at the age of 50; it can start at the age of 60 or 25, with the help of the students through student protest. This might be one of our tasks, so we can get some of the answers and provide some of the leadership for our institutions.

Richard Peairs:

There is some empirical data that shows that a faculty work week is a mean of about 55 hours, with a range from 22-to-74 hours. I don't mean to be apologetic, but there are a great number of members of the teaching profession who simply don't have time to become precinct workers. It's not quite that simple, I'm sure, but that may be one of the realities of the situation.

T. R. McConnell:

We're going to have to ration the time. I see many more hands. I'm going to try to get people who haven't spoken.

Floor:

I'd like to ask a question about the corporate institution position. I don't think anybody expects that a board of trustees of an institution can take a position on an issue like the Vietnam War. I'm not so sure that anybody cares. When it comes to the position of the university, a great university, I think there is a question as to what administrators are free, in a sense, and have the responsibility in quite another sense, of taking a position that they sincerely believe in.

I think we all agree that Berkeley is a great university. It's not because Berkeley has a great board of trustees. It may be because it has a great chancellor. It probably is because it has a great faculty, and possibly because it has some great, good administrators. Many of us here are administrators, and I'm concerned about what my responsibility is to myself to take a position. I'm not at all convinced that, even if the president of an institution took a position for or against the Vietnam War, that would stifle or in any way undercut the inquiry into that particular issue on his own campus. It think that's an important question.

T. R. McConnell:

There's somebody right behind you.

Floor:

This question has to do with the potential of social research or social change I'd like Dr. Boulding to comment on. I hear people saying that after we make recommendations, we leave them. I hear other people ask why the activists don't promote some sort of positive program for research. But as I've noticed what research has been done; currently it's been rejected by legislators and other people as not having any relevance or at least they don't see any relevance in it.

As we do the research, what are its potentials? It seems to me like you're asking the students to propose some sort of research for you to do, when they have no faith in research. What is the potential of social research for social change?

Kenneth Boulding:

I think one should not underestimate the cumulus of impact on people's images of the social system, of even the social sciences. Speaking as an economist, I think economics has made quite a dent in the last 30 or 40 years. We have not had a great depression, and with a bit of luck we won't. It isn't a bad idea to contrast the last 20 years with the 20 years between the two wars which were much worse. One reason for the generation gap is that my generation has been much more deeply traumatized than the younger generation. We've been through a hell of a lot more. Certainly. This generation under 30 has had all of its life on the rising market, and it was raised on the principles of Dr. Spock. My generation was raised on behaviorism, and was hit by two world wars and a great depression.

This is a real difference. It certainly is. What this means is that the world isn't going to be much better until we've died off. I think at the moment my generation is just a mass of scar tissue. We're just incapable of learning anything. One of the biggest evolutionary inventions, after all, was death. The best idea anybody ever had. I keep telling my young friends that the most important conflict in a war is usually against age.

We're a little too pessimistic sometimes. I do see some quite sizeable changes in the development of social self-conciousness. I'm even moderately optimistic about the international system. I think very profound changes are underway in the international system, which again have arisen out of the analytical capacities of the intellectual community.

We have a council of economic advisors. We don't have a council of international advisors so that nobody reads the bombing surveys. That's true. Give us a generation on this. Maybe we will have a council of international advisors, and maybe they'll have some good advice to give which would be even better. I'm optimistic Monday, Wednesday, and Friday, usually.

Floor:

I think that one of the problems is not the generation gap so much as it is an experience gap. And for Dr. Boulding to talk about having gone through the depression, which I did too, is all nice and very humorous, but I doubt that it makes very much of an impression on Mr. Jones or Mr. Ross.

What we're talking about has to do with perceptions of what are suggested and so forth, and what one perceives is based on one's experiences. We of the older generation know what what the problem is, but the people we're trying to get to perceive this — the students — don't see it because they didn't go through the depression.

Another thing which brings me to the main point here is the point that Dr. Johnson made this morning about integrity. This is his prime point. In integrity, we judge by other people's actions and our own experience. I have a feeling that what is being asked here by the young radicals, or the young students or whatever you want to call them, is to give them some signs of integrity which have meaning to them in light of their experiences.

There are many things which we as faculty members do, which probably do indicate a lack of integrity. We don't realize how clearly this lack of integrity is read by the younger generation. As a consequence, until we can develop some scheme to, first of all, act with integrity, and secondly, communicate the fact to the younger generation that we are acting with integrity, we might as well face up to it that we are going to have all sorts of difficulties. I'd like to know if this makes sense to you.

Kenneth Boulding:

I'd like to make a very brief comment on this. The primary purpose of the intellectual life is to liberate people from their own personal experiences.

T. R. McConnell:

There's a hand in the far corner.

Floor:

What I hear is a lot of intellectual tale-spinning. We're releasing a lot of energy and not sitting down in a group of 5 or 6 people with maybe a student, and I'm sorry. I can't see discussing social change without having a chief of police here, and a mayor here, and a city commissioner here. I can't see discussing social change — if you're discussing social change — without those people. I can't see it being done in a group of 125. You keep telling us that large universities don't work, large lectures aren't necessarily the best way to learn.

T. R. McConnell:

I want to recognize a gentleman whom I've disregarded before, be brief.

Floor:

There's been a reference to rebels without a program, and many a student has said this from the audience. I wonder if Mr. Ross will comment on that.

Robert Ross:

Yes. I don't think it's a serious position. All you have to do is listen to the students. They want a radical democratization of decision-making in the academic system of governments. They want drastically different kinds of relations to the apparatus of national defense and security. Many of them want the university that is explicitly committed to racial justice and poverty in the United States.

I don't think that that business about rebels without a program has any intellectual seriousness whatsoever. That is *New York Times* polemics by people who don't like disorder. There is a more serious problem. I was involved in some peace research projects that new left students created — very much on the inspiration of Kenneth Boulding. I don't believe we need more research to keep the United States out of counter-insurgency wars. We need to get out of those countries. A man argues that the university is the new church. And one of the liturgies of the new church is research, research, research, mumble, mumble, research. A lot of problems are political problems that don't require a lot of new knowledge. They require people to change their minds.

T. R. McConnell:

Does the professor wish to make a quick response?

Sir Peter:

I wonder if I could go back to the gentleman who made the, I thought, very pertinent remarks about integrity, and the communication of integrity, who was laughed out of court by a good intellectual crack. I really think he had a point. And I must say, as a senior academic administrator, in our system we're hybrids, whether we're fertile or not, of course, is another matter. But I must say that I, from my background of experience, am very troubled by some of the questions asked here tonight.

I thought the gentleman who early made the remarks about defensive positions was perfectly right. The whole tenor of presenting subjects inevitably in certain circumstances leads to defensiveness. And so one overcompensates. One has to be extremely careful about this, particularly in dealing with students. Clearly, in our situation, I assume it's the same in yours, they are members of the university. But one has to admit that many academics regard junior members as inferior members. This lack of integrity in relationship is caught, not taught. I don't think we deceive them.

My own experience of confrontation with the students was the first realization of this. The second consequence of it was to be saying to myself, and I hope to my colleagues, first of all: If two ships get on collision course, is all the error on one bridge? It might be on two bridges. I do assure you I'm not speaking here with any holier-than-thou attitudes. I'm trying to communicate to you what actually happened.

I addressed three meetings of students — probably 3,000 in all — and we were initially two groups of people shouting at each other across a void. There was no communication whatsoever until we could get into that situation of community with integrity, as the gentleman stressed. They certainly weren't believing us initially; we were too clever; we were professional; we were putting over the tricks fast. Until the basis of integrity was there and manifestly seen to be there, there was no possibility of progress.

I think this is one of the hardest things that the academic, after years of professional experience, has to learn because we're not scoring points. I'm trying to share with you an experience which, I can assure you, was a very significant one in my own professional life.

The second thing is that one must get away from the feeling that I am resolute, thou art firm, he is stubborn. Speaking scientifically, I am pure, thou art applied, he is technological. In the student situation, we could be saying that I have initiative but they are deviant.

It's this holy motive connotation of work in and efforts in certain directions to change the university, I hope through constitutional channels by constitutional means, which is somehow played out of court with a felt lack of integrity. I think the first duty I had, and my colleagues had, was to establish with the students a basis of talking together. This we managed over a period of five weeks. In the end, we established a working group to look — not simply at student representation on X and Y — but at the participation of members of the university and its work and life, which was much wider and took in the academics as well as the students and the lay people.

In contradistinction to many of the groups which have been set up in our country to discuss these matters, I'm happy to say in my case, the working group contains three lay members of the governing body, four academics, and four students. They are at work on this job of trying to look at the work and relationships of an institution which received the Royal Charter not four years ago. So much has the world changed.

I'm sure the gentleman who said that it must be with integrity, and it must manifestly be seen, to be there like justice, was on to a basic point.

T. R. McConnell:

These remarks, and some of the ones which just preceded Sir Peter's, lead me to make a comment.

We had several students at a faculty meeting not long ago, and the discussion lead me to say, "It's amazing how early the sense of infallibility develops." If I remember correctly, mine developed full-blown at about the same age and hasn't been reduced since.

I have been concerned, in a lingering way, with the discussion of the truth which was so prominent in the early session of this conference. I had an unhappy feeling that some of the discussants meant the truth. I had an unhappy feeling that *the* truth is something you start with, not something you pursue. I had an unhappy feeling that, when you start with the truth, the truth will determine the selection of staff and student and curriculum. I think I'd rather pursue it.

Finally, thinking of the sense of infallibility, which so many of us possess in generous degree, we should contemplate the truth with humility. I'm not at all sure that we know all we need to know to solve the world's problems. I am quite sure we don't. If we have learned anything recently, it is that these desperate problems that have been mentioned are extremely complex, and extremely difficult to solve. We badly need the fundamental knowledge with which to approach them. This means to me that this is the primary function of the university even if it has other functions. If we contemplate the truth with humility, we might remember what Whitehead said, "Nothing is more curious than the self-satisfied dogmatism with which mankind at each period of history cherished the delusion of the finality of its existing modes of knowledge, although I think there may be some revisionists in the group." And then Whitehead went on, apparently remembering what had happened to science in the past, "Einstein was supposed to have made an epochal discovery, I'm respectful and interested, but also skeptical. There is no more reason to suppose that Einstein's relativity is any more final than Newton's *Principia.*" The humility with which we ought to approach our task, it seems to me, is something I would like to remind myself.

BIBLIOGRAPHY

Aldrich, Winthrop W. *The University as an Instrument of Social Progress.* An address at Northeastern University, Boston, Mass., October 3, 1938. 13 pp.
An entreaty for greater cooperation between business and universities. Mr. Aldrich is particularly concerned about the dangers of a "planned economy," and it is against that prospect that he urges universities to prepare students.

American Assembly, The. *The Federal Government and Higher Education.* Englewood Cliffs, N. J.: Prentice-Hall, 1960.
A thorough analysis of the influence of the federal government on higher education made by a group of distinguished American scholars.

American Association of University Professors. *Depression, Recovery, and Higher Education.* New York: McGraw-Hill, 1937. 543 pp.
Primarily directed toward the encouragement of institutional research and comparative studies in higher education, this book does touch on the subject of this bibliography in Chapter 19, "Public Pressures and Higher Education," pp. 431-464.

American Council on Education. *Higher Education Cooperates in National Defense.* Washington, D.C.: ACE, 1941. 34 pp.
Shortly before Pearl Harbor, higher education in America moved to, in the words of the introduction, "review the work it has done so far and determine how it can best contribute in the future." Military defense, industrial defense, and civilian defense were all represented at the conference.

American Council on Education. *Higher Education in the National Service.* Washington, D.C.: ACE, 1950. 151 pp.
On page 79, Maj. Gen. Lewis Hershey states, "I am not going to labor the point, but the integration of our national defense and *you*—you people representing higher education—dare not, cannot, remain in the situation it is in now. We must dedicate ourselves to a future which will assure us that this greatest asset of ours stands ready, and every institution and every individual know the parts they are to play, whether the clouds are gone and the sun shines or whether the fog abounds—as it does today—or whether night sweeps over us. Whatever the future may bring, we must integrate and be ready."

Angell, James Rowland. *American Education: Essays and Articles.* New Haven: Yale University Press, 1937. 218 pp. James Angell presented these during his 1921-1937 tenure as president of Yale. A series of concise insights into higher education during a period of peace for America—insights, though, which span the activities of a university through prosperity and depression.

Association of American Universities. *The Rights and Responsibilities of Universities and Their Faculties*: A statement adopted March 24, 1953, and printed by the A.A.U. 11 pages.
"To enjoin uniformity of outlook upon a university faculty would put a stop to learning at its source. For these reasons a university does not take an official position of its own either on disputed questions of scholarship or on political questions or matters of public policy . . . membership in the Communist Party . . . extinguishes the right to a university position . . . if an instructor follows Communistic practice by becoming a propagandist for one opinion . . . he forfeits . . . his right to membership in the university."

Babbidge, Homer D. and Robert W. Rosenzweig. *The Federal Interest in Higher Education.* New York: McGraw-Hill, 1962. 214 pp.
Begins with a brief history then examines such issues as: contemporary policies and patterns, Congress, impact of programs, segregation, church and state, and federal control of education.

Beck, Hubert Park. *Men Who Control Our Universities.* New York: King's Crown Press, 1957. 229 pp.
Subtitled "The Economic and Social Composition of Governing Boards of Thirty Leading American Universities," in the first six chapters is discussed how the composition of governing boards tends to influence the character and the image of a university in society.

Benjamin, Harold R. W. *Higher Education in the American Republics.* New York: McGraw-Hill, 1965. 224 pp.
A comparative education textbook concentrating on the higher education of Anglo, Spanish, and Portuguese America.

Blackwell, Thomas Edward. *College Law: A Guide for Administrators.* Washington, D.C.: ACE, 1961. 347 pages.
A review of nearly all aspects of law as it affects the internal and external applications of university and college policy.

Bowman, Claude Charleton. *The College Professor in America.* Philadelphia: University of Pennsylvania Press, 1938. 196 pp.

A doctoral thesis which analyzes the articles by professors in general circulation magazines from the year 1890 to 1938. Of particular interest is Chapter 5, "The Professor in Political Affairs."

Brook, G. L. *The Modern University.* London: Andre Deutsch, 1965. 191 pp.

"Recent controversy has shown how few are the assumptions about the university that can count on general acceptance," says the author in the preface. He goes on to talk about the university despite the peril.

Clapp, Margaret (Ed.) *The Modern University.* Ithaca, N. Y.: Cornell University Press, 1950. 111 pp.

Four essays which point out the conflict of concepts within and between generations and countries, the victories and compromises of the 19th century that determined the nature of early 20th century universities and the problems that continue to face them.

Coffman, Lotus Delta. *Freedom Through Education.* Minneapolis: University of Minnesota Press, 1939. 56 pp.

Completed a few days before his death, this book was to have been his report, as president of the University of Minnesota, to the regents for the biennium 1938-39. All of the topics are presented in relation to the achievement of individual and social freedom through education.

Cohn, Alfred E. *Minerva's Progress: Tradition and Dissent in American Culture.* New York: Harcourt, Brace, and Co., 1946. 101 pp.

A discussion of "the circle; of what is known, what should be taught, and to what end" in our universities in the 20th century.

Committee on Government and Higher Education, The. *The Efficiency of Freedom.* Baltimore: Johns Hopkins Press, 1959. 44 pp.

Formed in 1957, the committee was handed the task of investigating fears that the legal autonomy of governing boards of public institutions was being eroded by state government. This is its report.

Compayre, Gabriel. *Abelard and the Origin and Early History of Universities.* New York: Charles Scribner's Sons, 1893. 315 pp.

The University of Paris is the central figure in this account, and the details of its early organization and influence are given. Its connection with the modern university is delineated. Abelard, whose system of teaching and disputation was one of the earliest signs of the rising universities, is the typical figure of the movement.

Conant, James B. and Francis T. Spaulding. *Educating for a Modern Society.* Cambridge, Mass.: Harvard University Graduate School of Education, 1940. 43 pp.

See especially the third and last of these three essays, Conant's "The Future of Our Higher Education," pages 27-43. In 1940 he saw American higher education as still predominantly aristocratic in nature, but looking to the future, he sees institutions assuming the responsibility of democratizing academia and the professions.

Curti, Merle and Roderick Nash. *Philanthropy in the Shaping of American Higher Education.* New Brunswick, N. J.: Rutgers University Press, 1965. 340 pp.

". . . But philanthropy as a shaping force had a special importance. In many cases it created the models that publicly supported universities and colleges later followed. Philanthropy financed the developments that helped make the tradition, and it paid for the implementation of policies, ideas, and theories."

Daniere, Andre. *Higher Education in the American Economy.* New York: Random House, 1964. 206 pp.

An economist's view of higher education. Much of the book is not directly relevant to the topic of this bibliography, but it does illustrate what the radical reformer of higher education will face if he tries to change universities without a close study of how the institution will fit into traditional economic frameworks.

Dent, H. C. *Universities in Transition.* London: Cohen and West, 1961. 176 pp.

"Universities have always been in transition . . . . The process of change has been unending because the universities have never failed to respond to the pressures, both internal and external, which have continuously been brought to bear upon them."

De Vane, William Clyde. *The American University in the Twentieth Century.* Baton Rouge: Louisiana State University Press, 1957. 72 pp.

Four papers presented as the Davis Washington Mitchell Lectures at Tulane University. They are "The University—Its Scope and Function," "The College," "The Liberating Studies," and "The University and the National Culture."

Dongerkery, S. D. *Universities and National Life*. Bombay, India: Hind Kitabs Ltd., 1950. 115 pp.

The author says, "Universities are an integral part of the life of the people. They cannot possibly lead an isolated existence. If they attempted to do so, they would wither and die." This book on emerging universities in India contains reviews of the Truman Commission on Higher Education for Democracy and the University Education Commission as seen through a foreigner's eyes.

Ducret, Bernard and Rafe-uz-Zaman. *The University Today: Its Role and Place in Society*. Geneva: World University Service, 1960. 333 pp.

See particularly chapter four of this study of higher education throughout the world, "Autonomy of the University."

Earnest, Ernest. *Academic Procession: An Informal History of the American College 1636 to 1953*. New York: Bobbs-Merrill, 1953.

"The history of the American college is an important chapter in the larger chronicle of the nation's cultural history. Reduced to its basic elements, this history is a record of a conflict between inherited tradition and the needs and desires of a restless dynamic society. The present study is an attempt to describe and evaluate both the tradition and the various forces opposed to it."

Eddy, Edward Danforth. *Colleges for Our Land and Time*. New York: Harper and Bros., 1957. 328 pp.

A history of the land-grant movement, prefaced by Russell I. Thackrey.

Eliot, Charles William. *Educational Reform: Essays and Addresses*. New York: The Century Co., 1905. 418 pp.

The speeches and essays of Charles William Eliot, president of Harvard, beginning with his inaugural address in 1869 and concluding with an address concerning the functions of education in a democratic society given in 1897. Of particular interest today is a brief speech entitled, "An Urban University," pages 395-398.

Elliott, Edward C. and M. M. Chambers. *Charters and Basic Laws of Selected American Universities and Colleges.* New York: The Carnegie Foundation, 1934. 640 pp.
This study includes 51 public and private institutions and relates, not only their charters regulating internal governance, but also federal and state laws and judicial decisions which affect them. A valuable reference.

Fairchild, Henry Pratt (Ed.) *The Obligation of Universities to the Social Order.* New York: New York University Press, 1933. 503 pp.
Seventy educators and intellectual leaders discuss the title topic from as many points of view.

Fehl, Noah Edward. *The Idea of a University in East and West.* Hong Kong: Chung Chi College Press, 1962. 402 pp.
A comparative, historical study of university education as it grew up in Eastern and Western civilization.

Ferguson, Charles. *The University Militant.* New York: Mitchell Kennerly, 1911. 184 pp.
A look six decades into the past which exhorts universities not to set themselves in opposition "to any of the existing arrangements of law or custom, but simply regard them as any other phenomena within the field of science."

Fine, Benjamin. *Democratic Education.* New York: Thomas Crowell Co., 1945. 251 pp.
An examination, just before the flood of post-war GI's, of the merits of the "aristocratic" and the "democratic" approaches to higher education in America. The author, education editor of the *New York Times* in 1945, illustrates the influence of higher education on America by examining the philosophies of St. John's at Annapolis and the University of Chicago.

Fischer, Joseph. *Universities in Southeast Asia.* Columbus, Ohio: Ohio State University Press, 1964. 133 pp.
"This monograph is a preliminary essay on the possible uses in underdeveloped countries of the university as a unit for social-science analyses. . . ."

Flexner, Abraham. *A Modern College and a Modern School.* Garden City, N. Y.: Doubleday, 1923. 142 pp.
These were originally two pamphlets, now published together in book form. The first provides an insight into the early movement within all higher education to "recognize the practical" in Amer-

ican life and to train students to practice in professions once not acceptable to academia. While Flexner encourages better education in the professions, he derides the setting of "standards that even the teachers can't meet."

Flexner, Abraham. *Universities: American, English, and German.* New York: Oxford University Press, 1930. 360 pp.
Flexner's comprehensive writings on the direction and content of university expansion continued. ". . . a university should not be a weather vane, responsive to every variation of popular whim. Universities must at times give society not what society wants, but what society needs."

Foerster, Norman (Ed.) *The Humanities After the War.* Princeton, N.J.: Princeton University Press, 1944. 95 pp.
Discussions of the title topic before the end of World War II by: Norman Foerster, Wendell Wilkie, Roscoe Pound, Theodore Greene, Abraham Flexner, William MacNeile Dixon, and Gordon Keith Chalmers.

Frankel, Charles (Ed.) *Issues in University Education.* New York: Harper and Bros., 1959. 175 pp.
Ten contemporary American scholars speak out on issues facing university education today. The sixth chapter, "The University and the Community," is of particular interest.

Fraser, Mowat G. *The College of the Future.* New York: Columbia University Press, 1937. 529 pp.
Subtitled "An Appraisal of Fundamental Plans and Trends in American Higher Education," this is an excellent, scholarly discussion of the de facto nonpartisan stance of the American university. Much of it is as applicable in 1968 as it probably was in 1937.

Gandhi, M. K. and others. *The Idea of a Rural University.* Sevagram: Hindustani Talimi Sangh, 1954. 102 pp.
See especially the 1st Chapter, "Higher Education," by Mahatma Ghandi.

Geyer, Denton L. *Current Issues in Education.* Chicago: Werkman's Book House, 1945. 92 pp.
Part III of this brief book is a history and analysis, pro and con, of federal aid to education. The analysis is made at a time when higher education's relationship to the federal government had just been vastly shifted due to World War II.

Gorovitz, Samuel. *Freedom and Order in the University.* Cleveland: Western Reserve University Press, 1967. 218 pp.
A discussion of the limits of internal restraints to be imposed by the university and the degree to which it should oppose restraints felt from outside. Includes contributions by Walter Metzger, John Searle, Sanford Kadish, and Paul Goodman.

Gould, Samuel B. *Knowledge is not Enough.* Yellow Springs, Ohio: The Antioch Press, 1959. 232 pp.
A collection of the speeches on higher education of a former president of Antioch, now president of the State University of New York.

Graham, Howard Jay and others. *The Students Speak Out.* New York: The New Republic, Inc., 1929. 269 pp.
Twenty-two students from as many colleges speak out on the improvement of their Alma Maters.

Harper, William Rainey. *The Trend in Higher Education.* Chicago: The University of Chicago Press, 1905. 390 pp.
"The University, I maintain, is the prophetic interpreter of democracy, the prophet of her past, in all its vicissitudes; the prophet of her present, in all its complexity; the prophet of her future, in all its possibilities . . . some (universities) are deaf to the cry of suffering humanity; some are exclusive and shut up within themselves; but the true university, the university of the future, is one the motto of which will be: Service for wherever mankind is, whether within scholastic walls . . . or in . . . the world at large."

Hartshorne, Edward Yarnall, Jr. *The German Universities and National Socialism.* Cambridge: Harvard University Press, 1937. 184 pages.
A prewar analysis of the place of the German university in shaping the Third Reich. "In the last analysis the monopolization of the liberal scientific university by the dogmatic totalitarian state has meant a renewed emphasis on *social,* at the expense of *intellectual,* values.

Hechinger, Fred. "What Should a University Be?" *AGB Reports.* June, 1966. pp. 20-21.
From an editorial in the *New York Times* and concerning a symposium at the Center for the Study of Democratic Institutions titled "The University in America."

Henderson, Algo D. "The Role of the Governing Board," *AGB Reports*. October, 1967. pp. 1-31 (entire edition).
"The lay board . . . has some advantages of involving representatives of the general public in the formation of policy . . . ."

Henry, David D. "Some Critical Issues in American Higher Education—the Public University," *AGB Reports*. June 1967, pp. 5-23.
The president of the University of Illinois takes a look at "who controls education?"

Howes, Raymond F. (Ed.) *Toward Unity in Educational Policy*. Washington, D.C.: ACE, 1953. 223 pp.
Of especial interest to the subject of this bibliography are three articles on pages 52-63. Presented to the annual ACE meeting in 1953, these papers speak of the dangers to the goals of colleges and universities as the McCarthy movement begins gaining full impetus. Also included are sections on ROTC and the implications of P.L. 550.

Husain, Zakir. *The Dynamic University*. London: Asia Publishing House, 1965. 117 pp.
Husain, vice-president of India, examines the responsibilities of higher education as he sees them in the India of the future.

Hutchins, Robert Maynard. *No Friendly Voice*. Chicago: The University of Chicago Press, 1936. 197 pp.
Addresses by one of America's best known advocates of the aloof, "objective," stance of liberal arts education.

International Student Conference. *The RIC Yearbook*. Rotterdam: Research and Information Commission of I.S.C., 1959. 160 pp.
A report on the status of academic freedom, particularly that affecting students, throughout the world in 1959.

Jacobsen, Ernest A. *Obligations of Higher Education to the Social Order*. Logan, Utah: The Faculty Association of Utah State Agricultural College, 1955. 31 pp.
"Changes in our society during the past half century have been phenomenal. Higher education has remained relatively static."

Jaspers, Karl. *The Idea of the University*. Boston: Beacon Press, 1959. 135 pp.
One of the eminent philosophers of the 20th century—an "ex-

istentialist" — examines higher education. Of particular interest is the final section, "State and Society."

Jones, Howard Mumford. *Education and World Tragedy.* Cambridge, Mass.: Harvard University Press, 1946. 178 pp.
"The values that may help our sick society will come, not from the dictates of specialism, but only as we have the courage in our colleges, so far as they can help, to face directly the tragic dilemma of our era."

Jordan, David Starr. *The Trend of the American University.* Palo Alto: Stanford University Press, 1929. 126 pp.
Concentrating on curriculum, these three essays show that evolvement of liberal education in the context of American social stress and on-campus conflicts concerning governance.

Kelly, Robert Lincoln. *The American College and the Social Order.* New York: The Macmillan Company, 1940. 380 pp.
"Since the ends the community seeks are usually very volatile, the colleges are called upon to assist in maintaining a balance of individual and social forces . . . . They have the function of serving as balance wheels . . . . They cannot be expected, chameleon-like, to change the color of their skins in response to every external stimulus or pressure."

Kennedy, Gail (Ed.) *Education for Democracy.* Boston: D. C. Heath and Co., 1952. 117 pp.
Readings representing points of view during the bitter debate which followed the release of the Report of the President's Commission on Higher Education.

Kerr, Clark. *The Uses of the Multiversity.* Cambridge, Mass: Harvard University Press, 140 pages, 1963.
"The university is being called upon to produce knowledge as never before—for civic and regional purposes, for national purposes. . ." A general scanning of the varied uses of the contemporary university and a justification for those uses.

Kibre, Pearl. *Scholarly Privileges in the Middle Ages.* Cambridge, Mass.: Mediaeval Academy of America, 1962. 446 pp.
An account of the rights, privileges, and immunities of scholars and universities at Bologna, Padua, Paris, and Oxford.

Kibre, Pearl. *The Nations in the Mediaeval Universities.* Cambridge, Mass.: Mediaeval Academy of America, 1958. 240 pp.
An analysis of "the corporation or association of masters, teaching all the arts, inscribed in the same role and living under the same laws, ordinances, and chiefs," otherwise known as nations. See particularly pp. 1-64.

Kirk, Grayson. "The University in Contemporary Society," *AGB Reports.* November, 1966. pp. 13-18.
"University leaders nowadays seldom are free from involvement in some public controversy. They must manage what is in reality a large business enterprise, but one that is dedicated to non-business purposes, and they must do so in a way that will be acceptable to four different publics." An excellent, short piece directed to the topic of this bibliography.

Kirkpatrick, J. E. *The American College and Its Rulers.* New York: New Republic, Inc., 1926. 309 pp.
An examination of college governance which in the end advocates "home rule" for colleges and abolition of absentee, "Tory" trustees. Chapters 13 and 14, "Students in Revolt-Militant Minorities on Campus," and "New Ventures-Cutting Loose from the Rotarians" are of interest.

Kirkpatrick, J. E. *Force and Freedom in Education.* Yellow Springs, Ohio: The Antioch Press, 1929. 128 pp.
The author attempted, four decades ago, to show "that our present school system belongs, both in theory and practice, to an earlier age, that it embodies few democratic principles, little that is useful and much that is harmful to a democratic society. It is further suggested that what we now have is not education at all, merely instruction and discipline, mass schooling in the interest of the status quo . . . . "

Knight, Edgar W. *What College Presidents Say.* Chapel Hill, N.C.: The University of North Carolina Press, 1940. 377 pp.
Completed in 1939, this book is an attempt through quotation and paraphrasing to show how college presidents look at the responsibilities of higher education. Section 6 is entitled "Obligations to Society" and contains such subject headings as: General Principles; The Lower Schools; The Education of Women; The Education of the Negro; The Effect of the World War; Adult Education; Federal Relations; and Gentlemen of the Graduating Class.

Leach, A. F. *Educational Charters and Documents 598-1909*. Cambridge, England: Cambridge University Press, 1911. 582 pp.
The legal documents relating to British schools over a period of 13 centuries.

Leland Stanford Junior University. *The University and the Future of America*. Palo Alto: Stanford University Press, 1941. 274 pp.
A symposium during the Fiftieth Anniversary of Stanford including educators and intellectual leaders from throughout the U.S.— pre-Pearl Harbor.

Lilge, Frederic. *The Abuse of Learning: the Failure of the German University*. New York: The Macmillan Company, 1948. 184 pp.
"By studying the ideas and ideals that inspired, directed, and finally corrupted the teaching of these universities, I hope to shed some light on the way which, in little more than a century, has led from the noble dignity of the brothers Humboldt to the degraded life which today creeps in the ruined German cities."

Lunden, Walter A. *The Dynamics of Higher Education*. Pittsburgh: The Pittsburgh Printing Company, 1939. 402 pp.
A sociological analysis of the history of higher education as a social institution.

Madsen, David. *The National University*. Detroit: Wayne State University Press, 1966. 178 pp.
A history of the concept of a "national" university from colonial times to the present.

Marsh, Clarence Stephen (Ed.) *Organizing Higher Education for National Defense*. Washington D.C.: ACE, 1941. 67 pages.
Papers from a conference held ten months before Pearl Harbor illustrate the beginning of a since increasing involvement of higher education in the military sector. Brigadier General Lewis B. Hershey was a speaker. He concludes, "but there must be for the good of the country and for the good of the colleges a large representation from college personnel at all times in our defense forces."

Mayer, Frederick. *Creative Universities*. New York: College and University Press, 1961. 111 pp.

"To preserve mankind, universities must not only mirror the dominant currents of society, but they must also be beacons of enlightenment so that society can become more rational and humane."

McAllister, Charles E. *Inside the Campus: Mr. Citizen Looks at His Universities.* New York: Fleming Revell Co., 1958. 247 pp.
A president of the Association of Governing Boards takes a look at American higher education in order to explain to citizens the realities of everything from teaching load to Communism on campus.

Meland, Bernard Eugene. *Higher Education and the Human Spirit.* Chicago: University of Chicago Press, 1953. 204 pp.
The author contends that the duty of higher education goes beyond the imparting of objective knowledge and into the obligations of a spiritual and moral nature. To do so would imply that higher education must be possessed of a moral or spiritual stance. This book is an attempt to evaluate the willingness of higher education to both assume and succeed in such a stance.

Melby, Ernest O., Andrew Conway Ivy, Franklin Porter Graham. *Higher Learning and the World Crisis.* Washington, D.C.: NEA, 1948. 22 pp.
Three addresses, one by each of the three listed authors. The first, "The Role of the University in Building World Peace," begins, "Universities are among our oldest social institutions. Speaking generally, they have characteristically been indifferent to their social responsibilities . . . not infrequently they have viewed questions of social policy as practical matters which lie outside of the rightful concern of the university."

Mill, John Stuart. *Inaugural Address.* London: Longmans, Green, Reader and Dyer, 1867. 99 pp.
The new honorary president of the University of St. Andrews delivers in his inaugural speech a comprehensive portrayal of his philosophy of education.

Miller, J. Hillis and Dorothy Brocks. *The Role of Higher Education in War and After.* New York: Harper and Bros., 1944. 222 pp.
In relation to the topic of this bibliography see particularly Chapter 8, "The Responsibility for Civilian Morale."

Moberly, Sir Walter. *The Crisis in the University*. London: SCM Press Ltd., 1949. 316 pp.

A post-World War II writer addresses himself to the question "Can universities adapt themselves to a world of insecurity?" . . . "All familiar questions of policy . . . require to be rethought in the new perspective." See pp. 30-49 and 225-260.

Neilson, William Allen and Carl Frederick Witte. *The Function of Higher Education*. Evanston, Illinois: Northwestern University Press, 1943. 64 pp.

Two lectures on the function of the university and of the liberal arts college, given in the context of World War II and the exodus of professors to Washington and war.

Nevins, Allan. *The State Universities and Democracy*. Urbana: University of Illinois Press, 1962. 171 pp.

These lectures, delivered at the University of Illinois to mark the centennial of the Morrill Act, are an examination of the development of state and land-grant institutions in four stages.

Newman, John Henry Cardinal. *The Idea of a University*. New York: Longmans, Green and Co., 1929. 519 pp.

A classic in the history of higher education, which, if not addressed directly to the subject of this bibliography, provides a starting point for more contemporary doctrines attempting to relate the university to society.

Newsom, Carroll V. *A University President Speaks Out*. New York: Harper and Bros., 1961. 115 pp.

An educator and college president speaks on the accumulation of 25 years of experience in colleges and universities, touching many times upon the topic of this bibliography.

Niblett, W. R. *The Expanding University*. London: Faber and Faber, 1962. 132 pp.

A report on a conference held at Oxford in 1961 at which the contributors "were aware that the real problems of the expanding university are . . . concerned with (its) fundamental obligations both to (its) students and to society."

Norton, Arthur O. *Readings in the History of Education: Mediaeval Universities*. Cambridge: Harvard University Press, 1909. 153 pp.

This book is a general history of the mediaeval university. Of interest to the subject of this bibliography are pages 80-101 dealing with university privileges relating to sovereigns, the law, taxation, and municipalities.

President's Commission on Higher Education, The. *Higher Education for American Democracy*. New York: Harper and Bros., 1947.
Included in this book are all six of the volumes covering the various elements of the report of the Commission. Of particular interest is the first volume, "Establishing the Goals."

Pritchett, Henry Smith. *The Spirit of the State Universities*. Reprint from the University of California Chronicle, Volume XII, No. 2, 1910. 26 pp.
An address delivered at the Charter Day Exercises, University of California, 1910. "The state university of fifty years ago was launched upon the uncertain sea of politics. It has been a part of the work of every state university to educate the people of its state to the conception that partisan politics could not be mixed into the administration of a university without poisoning the very spirit for which it stood. It took years for this lesson to be learned."

Reeves, Marjorie (Ed.) *Eighteen Plus, Unity and Diversity in Higher Education*. London: Faber and Faber, 1965. 226 pp.
See particularly Part One, "Higher Education and Society." Concerns British higher education.

Riedl, John O. *The University in Process*. Milwaukee: Marquette University Press, 1965. 78 pp.
The Aquinas Lecture delivered at Marquette compares universities in American society with other "fundamental associations," i.e., industrial corporations, government, research foundations, churches, etc.

Robbins, Lord. *The University in the Modern World*. New York: St. Martin's Press, 1966. 157 pp.
A look at the changing responsibilities and functions of British higher education.

Root, E. Merrill. *Collectivism on the Campus: The Battle for the Mind in American Colleges*. New York: Devin-Adair Co., 1956. 403 pp.
The author on p. 19, "Even if there are no outright Communists on a faculty, the non-Communists often have been so condition-

ed by the Communist minority of American intellectuals, outside the college as well as inside, that they know not what they do." And it goes on and on revealing plot after plot in American colleges and universities but concludes on a note of hope with a chapter titled, "Toward a New Destiny."

Roper, Elmo. *The Public Looks at Higher Education.* Prepared for *Fortune Magazine,* June, 1949. 311 pp.
This study is "in some sense . . . a measure of the strength of the popular belief that education is a primary means to social and economic advancement." The study as it appears before publication in *Fortune* is in typed and mimeographed form, and its distribution is thus likely to be quite limited.

ROTC Study Committee of Colgate University. *The Impact of an ROTC Program on a Liberal Arts College: A Case Study at Colgate University.* Hamilton N. Y.: Colgate University, 1953. 53 pp.
The foreword opens, "Is there a place in the liberal arts curriculum for military studies of a technical and professional nature? Are the objectives of civilian and military studies compatible? If so, how are the two to be articulated?"

Russell, James Earl. *Federal Activities in Higher Education After World War II.* New York: King's Crown Press, 1957. 253 pp.
"An analysis of the nature, scope, and impact of federal activities in higher education in the fiscal year 1957." An appendix of more than 100 pages illustrates the involvement of higher education governmental goals in the immediate post-war years.

Russell, John Dale. *Emergent Responsibilities in Higher Education.* Chicago: University of Chicago Press, 1946. 142 pp.
See in particular: "Historic Relationships of Colleges and Universities to the Communities and Societies in Which They Have Flourished," beginning on p. 40 and written by Newton Edwards.

Seeley, the Reverend R. S. K. *The Function of the University.* New York: Oxford University Press, 1948. 79 pp.
A brief look at the changing commitments of Canadian higher education in the immediate post-war period, an emphasis on Catholic education.

Sinclair, Upton. *The Goose Step*. Pasadena: Upton Sinclair,
1923. 488 pp.
A scathing indictment, by the noted reform writer, of American
higher education following World War I. Indexed.

Smith, Huston. *The Purposes of Higher Education*. New York:
Harper and Bros., 1955. 218 pp.
An interdisciplinary, and highly intellectually oriented, look at
what the future aims of higher education should be—from the
vantage point of 1955.

Stanley, George and Guy Sylvestre. *Canadian Universities
Today*. Toronto: University of Toronto Press, 1961. 97 pp.
Papers presented to the Royal Society of Canada during its an-
nual symposium in 1960. The second paper, "The Responsibility
of the Universities," and the last, "Australian Universities: A
Comparison," are of particular interest.

Taylor, Harold. *On Education and Freedom*. New York:
Abelard-Schuman, 1954. 320 pp.
The final chapter of this book, written during the McCarthy era,
is an excellent examination of the question of partisanship by
universities in issues causing social upheaval. The chapter is
entitled "Communism and American Democracy" and is an
eloquent defense of neutrality following the statement of the
A.A.U. concerning the same issue which threw that organization
squarely on one side of the McCarthy issue.

Veblen, Thorstein. *The Higher Learning in America, A
Memorandum on the Conduct of Universities by Business-
men*. New York: Sagamore Press, 1957. 209 pp.
Written in the early twentieth century. Introduction by Louis
Hacker.

Vesey, Laurence R. *The Emergence of the American University*. Chicago: The University of Chicago Press, 1965. 505
pp.
An intellectual history of the American university from 1865-
1910.

Walden, John W. H. *The Universities of Ancient Greece*. New
York: Charles Scribner's Sons, 1909. 367 pages.
See in particular pages 58-67, "Education and the State," and
pages 109-129, "The Decline of University Education: The
Conflict with Christianity."

Weidner, Edward W. *The World Role of Universities*. New York: McGraw-Hill, 1962. 366 pp.
A critique of the American university as agent of social change in foreign societies through projects carried out there.

Wiggins, Sam P. *The Desegregation Era in Higher Education*. Berkeley, California: McCutchan Publishing Corporation, 1966. 106 pp.
An analysis of the degree of success toward desegregation in southern institutions of higher learning.

Wilson, Howard E. and Florence H. Wilson. *American Higher Education and World Affairs*. Washington, D.C.: ACE, 1963. 158 pp.
"Mr. and Mrs. Wilson's . . . volume brings together the threads of preceding studies. Their primary emphasis, however, is not so much a summary as an analysis of institutional policy and administrative organization by which policy may be implemented."

Witmer, Lightner. *The Nearing Case*. New York: B. W. Huebsch, 1915. 123 pp.
The documents surrounding the dismissal of an associate professor at the University of Pennsylvania in 1915, allegedly because Nearing favored child labor laws opposed by members of the state legislature who controlled appropriations to the university.

Yen, Maria. *The Umbrella Garden*. New York: The Macmillan Company, 1954. 268 pp.
Subtitled "A Picture of Student Life in Red China." This book is a thinly veiled condemnation of the part played by Chinese academic communities and their members in aiding the advance of Mao Tse Tung into mainland cities.

Zweig, Michael. *The Idea of a World University*. Carbondale, Ill.: Southern Illinois University Press, 1967. 204 pp.
A proposal for international higher education in which no single cultural, national or political bloc dominates the curriculum.

PUBLISHED PAPERS from PREVIOUS

COLLEGE and UNIVERSITY

SELF-STUDY INSTITUTES

College Self-Study: Lectures on Institutional Research, Given at Stanford University, July 19-25, 1959, Richard G. Axt and Hall T. Sprague, eds. Available through Inter-library Loan Service from the depository libraries listed on page 148.

Research on College Students: Institute Lectures Considering Recent Research on College Students' Motivation, Values and Attitudes, and Campus Cultures, 1960, Hall T. Sprague, ed. Available through Inter-library Loan Service.

Studies of College Faculty: The Papers Presented at the Institute for College and University Administrators and Faculty, 1961. Available through Inter-library Loan Service.

The Study of Campus Cultures: The Papers Presented at the Fourth Annual Institute on College Self-Study, 1962. Terry F. Lunsford, ed. Xerographic copies are available from University Microfilms, Inc., 313 N. 1st St., Ann Arbor, Mich. 48103. $6.65. Also available through Inter-library Loan Service.

The Study of Academic Administration: Papers Presented at the Fifth Annual Institutes on College Self-Study, 1963. Terry F. Lunsford, ed. Xerographic copies are available from University Microfilms, Inc., 313 N. 1st St., Ann Arbor, Mich. 48103. $6.65. Also available through Inter-library Loan Service.

Long-Range Planning in Higher Education: The Papers and Discussions of the Sixth Annual Institute on College Self-Study for College and University Administrators, 1964, Owen A. Knorr, ed. Available through WICHE. $3.00.

Order and Freedom on the Campus: Rights and Responsibilities of Faculty and Students. Seventh Annual Institute on College Self-Study for College and University Administrators. 1965, Owen A. Knorr and W. John Minter, eds. Available through WICHE. $3.50.

Campus and Capitol: Higher Education and the State. Papers from the Eighth Annual College Self-Study Institute, 1966, W. John Minter, ed. Available through WICHE. $3.50.

The Individual and the System: Personalizing Higher Education. Papers from the Ninth Annual Institute on College Self-Study, 1967, W. John Minter, ed. Available through WICHE. $3.50.

Depository Libraries

University of Alaska Library
College, Alaska 99735

University of Arizona Library
Tucson, Arizona 55721

University of California Library
Berkeley, California 94720

University of California Library
Los Angeles, California 90024

Norlin Library
University of Colorado
Boulder, Colorado 80302

Gregg M. Sinclair Library
University of Hawaii
Honolulu, Hawaii 96822

University of Idaho Library
Moscow, Idaho 83843

University of Montana Library
Missoula, Montana 59801

University of Nevada Library
Reno, Nevada 89507

University of New Mexico Library
Albuquerque, New Mexico 87106

University of Oregon Library
Eugene, Oregon 97403

University of Utah Library
Salt Lake City, Utah 84112

University of Washington Library
Seattle, Washington 98105

University of Woyming Library
Laramie, Wyoming 82070

Graduate School of Education Library
Lawrence Hall
Harvard University
Cambridge Massachusetts 02138

Teachers College Library
525 West 120th St.
New York, New York 10027

25:4M:1168:dwi:PP:2B40